American Wake-Up Call

Barry Robbins

Copyright © 2024 Barry Robbins

Cover art: Barry Robbins/Awan Designer

All rights reserved

No part of this book may be reproduced in any form or by any electronic or mechanical means, including information storage and retrieval systems, without written permission from the author, except in the case of a reviewer, who may quote brief passages embodied in critical articles or in a review. The views and the opinions expressed in this book are those of the author. All content provided is not intended to malign any religion, ethnic group, club, organization, company, or individual.

Printed in the United States of America

Title: American Wake-Up Call

Author: Barry Robbins

Paperback ISBN: 979-8-9897678-9-2

Dedication

To Pam, my caregiver extraordinaire, without whom this work would not have been possible. Words cannot express my gratitude.

Contents

Introduction	1
Part One: Critical Challenges	3
1. The Paralysis of Power Edward Gibbon on America's Crisis of Capability	5
2. Breaking Down the Walls Nelson Mandela on American Division	10
3. The Burden of Presumed Greatness Tocqueville on American Arrogance	15
4. The Broken Oath Hippocrates on the American Healthcare System	20
5. Arms and Anarchy Alexander Hamilton on Gun Violence in America	24
6. The Rigged Game Theodore Roosevelt on American Inequality	28
7. The New Industrial Servitude Frances Perkins on Worker Rights	32

8.	The Great Disruption	36
	Alexander von Humboldt on America's Climate Impact	
9.	The Failed Promise	41
	Horace Mann on American Education	
10.	The Tyranny of Ignorance	45
	John Stuart Mill on American Democracy	
11.	The Price of the Ticket	49
	James Baldwin on American Racism	
12.	The Republic in Peril	53
	George Washington on Political Violence	
13.	Democracy for Sale	57
	Louis Brandeis on Money in Politics	
14.	The Warning Unheeded	61
	Eisenhower on the Military-Industrial Complex	
15.	A System in Chaos	65
	Jane Addams on America's Immigration Failure	
16.	Wires and Lights in Darkness	69
	Edward R. Murrow on America's Media Crisis	
17.	A House Divided	73
	John Marshall on the Supreme Court	
18.	Living Beyond Our Means	77
	Andrew Jackson on the National Debt	
Part Two: Systemic Problems		81

19.	An Obsolete Compromise James Madison on the Electoral College	83
20.	The Dead Hand Jefferson on America's Constitutional Crisis	87
21.	Houses Without Homes Jane Jacobs on America's Housing Crisis	91
22.	The Great Stagnation Baron Haussmann on America's Infrastructure Crisis	96
23.	Medicine vs. Handcuffs William Halsted on America's Drug Policy	101
24.	The New Asylum Dorothea Dix on America's Mental Health Crisis	106
25.	The New Jungle Upton Sinclair on America's Food System	110
26.	The Illusion of Justice Cesare Beccaria on America's Death Penalty	115
27.	In the Dark Carl Sagan on America's War Against Science	120
28.	A Matter of Measure Condorcet on America's Metric Resistance	124
29.	Machines Without Morals Norbert Wiener on AI Management	128

30. The Willing Prisoners — 132
George Orwell on Digital Surveillance

31. The Law's Burden — 136
Oliver Wendell Holmes Jr. on America's Litigation Obsession

32. Stone Age Banking — 140
J.P. Morgan on America's Financial Infrastructure

Part Three: Lighter Side — 145

33. A Fixed Predicament — 147
Mark Twain on America's Shower Head Folly

34. Clean Habits and Closed Minds — 151
Benjamin Franklin on America's Bidet Aversion

35. The Important Art of Keeping One's Card — 155
Oscar Wilde on American Restaurant Payments

36. The Patient-Doctor — 159
Molière on America's Pharmaceutical Advertising

37. The Path Forward — 163
Finding Hope in Hard Truths

Also by Barry Robbins — 167

About the author — 169

Introduction

What if we could consult history's greatest minds about America's current problems?

Imagine Hippocrates examining our healthcare system, Alexander Hamilton addressing gun violence, or Nelson Mandela analyzing our social divisions. What insights would they offer? What solutions might they propose?

This book attempts exactly that. By channeling historical figures who dealt with similar challenges or possessed relevant expertise, we gain fresh perspectives on America's most pressing problems. These voices were chosen not for their fame but for their unique qualifications to address specific issues. Hippocrates revolutionized medicine's ethical framework. Hamilton helped create America's federal system. Mandela healed a deeply divided nation.

Some might question this approach. After all, these historical figures couldn't have known about today's specific challenges. But that's precisely the point. Their distance from our current situation, combined with their relevant experience, allows them to see patterns and possibilities we might miss. They offer the wisdom of hindsight combined with the authority of experience.

The book is organized in three parts. Part One examines critical challenges threatening America's future. Part Two analyzes systemic problems that undermine our effectiveness. Part Three looks at seemingly minor issues that nevertheless reveal something important about our national character.

These historical voices don't always agree with each other. They sometimes propose conflicting solutions. That's as it should be—America's problems are complex and reasonable people can differ on solutions. What matters is gaining new perspectives on persistent problems.

The goal isn't to provide easy answers but to help us think differently about our challenges. Perhaps by listening to voices from the past, we can find new paths forward.

Part One: Critical Challenges

Chapter 1
The Paralysis of Power
Edward Gibbon on America's Crisis of Capability

As the historian who chronicled the decline and fall of Rome in my life's work, I have a particular sensitivity to the patterns by which great powers lose their ability to meet challenges. When I spent two decades documenting how Rome descended from the height of its powers into dysfunction and decay, I never imagined I would witness similar patterns in the modern world's greatest republic. Yet here we are: the United States, possessed of unprecedented wealth, technology, and human capital, finds itself increasingly unable to solve even basic problems, let alone address the great challenges of its age.

The Patterns of Decline

The parallels between Rome's decay and America's dysfunction are striking. In Rome, I documented how a great power could retain all the trappings of strength while losing its ability to solve problems or meet challenges. Today, I observe an America that can launch rockets into space but cannot fix its public schools, that can develop vaccines in record time but cannot ensure their distribution, that can project military power globally but cannot secure its own borders.

Like Rome in its declining years, America maintains the outward appearance of power while its problem-solving capabilities atrophy. Climate change threatens, yet no coherent response emerges. Infrastructure crumbles while endless reports are written. Healthcare costs spiral while known solutions remain unimplemented. Education declines while reforms are endlessly debated. The national debt grows while both parties avoid hard choices. Gun violence continues while meaningful action is blocked.

The Mechanics of Dysfunction

In Rome, I observed how institutional decay followed predictable patterns. First came the loss of shared truth—when citizens could no longer agree on basic facts, they could not agree on solutions. Then followed the erosion of civic virtue, where private interest overwhelmed public good. Finally arrived the death of institutional effectiveness, where systems designed to solve problems instead perpetuated them.

America's institutions now exhibit hauntingly similar dysfunction. Congress produces theatre instead of legislation. Regulatory agencies are captured by those they should regulate. Courts become political battlegrounds. State and federal governments engage in endless conflict. Bureaucracies sustain problems rather than solve them. The machinery of government still operates, but it no longer produces results.

The Corruption of Purpose

In Rome's decline, I documented how money gradually corrupted every institution's original purpose. America faces similar corruption, though through more sophisticated mechanisms. Lobbying has transformed legislation from problem-solving to profit protection. Campaign finance has turned representatives into full-time fundraisers. Revolving doors between industry and government have blurred the line between public and private interests. Short-term profit considerations routinely override long-term national needs.

But money is merely a symptom of deeper dysfunction. The fundamental problem is the loss of institutional capacity—the ability to identify challenges, develop solutions, and implement them effectively. America retains enormous strength but increasingly lacks the ability to use that strength purposefully.

The Death of Competence

Perhaps most alarming is the deterioration in leadership quality. In Rome, I observed how the skills needed to obtain power became divorced from those needed to exercise it wisely. America now faces a similar crisis. Political success requires skills entirely unrelated to governance. Ideology trumps expertise. Loyalty overshadows competence. Performance matters less than perception. Short-term thinking replaces long-term planning.

The result is leadership incapable of addressing complex challenges, even when solutions are known and resources available. Like Rome in its later years, America finds itself led by those who excel at gaining power but lack the wisdom to use it effectively.

The Path to Renewal

Yet unlike Rome, America's dysfunction need not be terminal. The recognition of systemic failure can, if properly understood, guide reformation. Your institutions must be freed from capture by special interests and restored to their original purposes. Your civic capacity for evidence-based solution-building must be rebuilt. Mechanisms favoring long-term thinking over short-term gains must be created. Systems for selecting leaders must prioritize competence over ideology and fundraising ability.

Most fundamentally, you must reconstruct the ability to establish shared facts and truth, without which no problem-solving is possible. A society that cannot agree on basic reality cannot address complex challenges.

A Final Warning

When I wrote of Rome's decline, I noted that it happened gradually, then suddenly. Systems appear to function until they decisively fail. America approaches such a moment of truth.

Remember: Rome fell not from lack of power, but from inability to use that power effectively. It retained the appearance of greatness long after losing the capacity for renewal and reform. Your republic retains enormous strength, but strength without the ability to apply it effectively becomes mere spectacle—impressive but ultimately futile.

The choice before you is clear: reform your capacity to solve problems, or join the long list of great powers that retained all the trappings of strength while losing the ability to meet the challenges that ultimately destroyed them. The chapters that follow will examine specific manifestations of this systemic dysfunction, but understand: these are not separate problems. They are symptoms of a deeper crisis—the loss of America's basic ability to solve problems and meet challenges.

Chapter 2
Breaking Down the Walls
Nelson Mandela on American Division

When I walked out of prison after 27 years, many expected—perhaps even hoped—that I would call for vengeance. Instead, I called for reconciliation. Today, I look at your divided America and see both parallels to our struggle and, more importantly, paths to healing that you have yet to explore.

The Nature of Your Division

In South Africa, we faced apartheid—legal, physical separation. Your divisions may lack the formal structure of apartheid, but they are no less real. You have created invisible but powerful walls throughout your society that are just as effective at preventing human connection. Your news channels tell entirely different stories about the same events, creating separate realities for different groups. Your social media platforms construct bubbles that never intersect, reinforcing existing beliefs while blocking contrary views. Your neighborhoods increasingly sort themselves by political belief, creating geographical separation as real as any apartheid law.

The segregation extends into every aspect of life. Your schools grow more segregated by class and race. Your workplaces become zones where certain views cannot be safely expressed. Even your families can no longer gather for holidays because of political differences. This is not the formal separation of apartheid, but its effect is the same—the death of empathy and understanding.

Learning from South Africa

Let me share something I learned during my twenty-seven years in prison. My jailers arrived believing I was a dangerous terrorist. I could have confirmed their fears, treated them with the hatred they expected. Instead, I chose a different path. I learned their language, studied their culture, talked to them about their families. Gradually, they began to see me as human. Some even became allies in our cause.

This taught me a crucial lesson: People are not born hating each other. They learn to hate. And if they can learn to hate, they can be taught to love. This insight guided our nation's healing and holds the key to addressing your divisions today.

The Cost of Division

Your polarization exacts a terrible price that many Americans have yet to fully recognize. Communities lose the diversity that drives innovation and growth. Children grow up fearing and suspecting "the other side," inheriting divisions they did not create. Democracy itself weakens as compromise becomes impossible and basic governance fails. Your economy suffers as cooperation breaks down and shared enterprises become impossible. Even your national security is compromised when internal unity dissolves.

In South Africa, we faced these same challenges. The costs of division threatened to destroy our nation. But we found a way forward, and so can you.

The Path to Healing

Drawing from our experience with the Truth and Reconciliation Commission and my personal journey from prisoner to president, I see clear steps America must take. First, you must create spaces for truth-telling—not for political debate, but for sharing personal stories. When we created such forums in South Africa, both victims and perpetrators could speak their truth. When people share their fears and hopes directly, demonization becomes harder.

Second, build common projects that require cooperation across political lines. We rebuilt our communities with blacks and whites working side by side. When people build together, they learn to respect each other. The project itself becomes less important than the connections it creates.

Third, reform your information ecosystem that currently profits from division. Create incentives for journalism that bridges divides rather than deepens them. In South Africa, our healing required all sides to hear the same facts, even if they interpreted them differently.

Fourth, teach active reconciliation in your schools. It is not enough to preach tolerance; young people must learn how to disagree without disconnecting, how to challenge ideas without attacking people. These are skills that must be taught and practiced.

Fifth, use the unifying power of sports and culture. Remember how the Rugby World Cup helped unite South Africa? Create more cultural and sporting events that bring people together. Shared joy is a powerful antidote to division.

A Personal Approach

Let me share a strategy I used with those who opposed me most fiercely. I would say: "*I understand your fears. They are human. But let us talk about our hopes—they may be more similar than you think.*" This approach opens doors that confrontation keeps firmly closed.

In your own lives, take small steps. Invite someone from "the other side" to coffee. Listen to understand, not to respond. Share personal stories rather than political arguments. Find one small point of agreement and build from there. Focus on the future you both want for your children.

A Final Word

During our struggle, we had a saying: "*Unity is strength, division is weakness.*" But unity does not mean uniformity. It means finding ways to work together despite differences. America, your situation is not hopeless. I have seen people overcome far deeper divisions. But you must choose this path. As I once said, "*It always seems impossible until it is done.*"

Remember: When I became President, I could have sought revenge. Instead, I invited my former jailers to the inauguration.

They came, and they wept. Change is possible, but it requires the courage to take the first step toward those you fear or mistrust.

The choice is yours. You can remain in your separate camps, growing further apart, or you can begin the hard but rewarding work of reconciliation. As we say in South Africa: *"Ubuntu"—"I am because we are."*

The future of your republic depends not on defeating the other side, but on rediscovering your common humanity.

Chapter 3

The Burden of Presumed Greatness

Tocqueville on American Arrogance

When I traveled across America in 1831, documenting your young democracy for my work "Democracy in America," I observed a unique national characteristic: a profound belief in American exceptionalism. This belief had its uses then—it gave your young nation confidence to experiment with democracy on a scale never before attempted. But today, I observe how this same characteristic has calcified into something more troubling: an arrogance that blinds America to both its faults and others' virtues.

The Evolution of Exceptionalism

In my time, I wrote that "*Americans are so enamored of equality that they would rather be equal in slavery than unequal in freedom.*" Today, I might write that Americans are so enamored of their own superiority that they would rather fail their own way than succeed someone else's. This is not mere pride; it is a peculiar form of willful ignorance that prevents learning from others' experiences.

I watch with dismay as your healthcare system falters while you refuse to learn from other nations' successes. Your cities choke in traffic while you dismiss European public transportation solutions. Your schools decline while you ignore proven educational methods from Asia. Your children die from gun violence while you reject proven safety measures that work elsewhere. Your inequality grows while you disclaim Nordic social policies that have created more equitable societies.

The Peculiar American Mind

In 1831, I observed that Americans had developed certain habits of mind. Some were admirable: practicality, industriousness, optimism. But I also noted a tendency toward intellectual self-satisfaction that has only grown worse. You have developed an assumption that being American automatically confers expertise, that American solutions must be superior simply because they are American, that American failures are somehow preferable to foreign successes.

This manifests most clearly in international forums, where American representatives display what one might call "diplomatic deafness"—an inability to hear wisdom in foreign accents. Power has bred not wisdom but an assumption that wisdom is unnecessary.

The Cost of Ignorance

The price of this arrogance extends far beyond wounded international relationships. Valuable opportunities for learning are lost. International cooperation becomes impossible when one party refuses to listen. Proven solutions to serious problems are ignored simply because they originated elsewhere. Allies grow weary of American lectures about American superiority. Progress on global challenges stalls because the world's most powerful nation refuses to learn from others' experiences.

When I wrote about America's potential greatness, I never imagined that potential would become its own obstacle. Yet here we are: American exceptionalism has become exceptional mainly in its ability to prevent America from learning from others.

The Sources of Arrogance

The roots of this problem run deep in American history and geography. Your continent-spanning country, bounded by oceans, has bred both independence and ignorance of others. Victory in World War II and the Cold War created an assumption of perpetual superiority that persists despite mounting evidence to the contrary. Your media and education systems rarely look outward except in crisis, creating a culturally insular population. English's role as a global language has made Americans uniquely monolingual among developed nations, further isolating them from global perspectives.

Most perniciously, past economic success has bred an assumption of perpetual leadership that makes learning from others seem unnecessary. This creates a self-reinforcing cycle: ignorance of other nations breeds assumption of superiority, which breeds resistance to learning, which breeds increased ignorance.

The Path to Wisdom

When I studied America, I found much to admire. That admiration compels me to suggest necessary reforms. Your education system must prioritize international awareness and foreign language study—an American who speaks only English is wearing intellectual blinders. You must create more opportunities for Americans to study and work abroad, as nothing cures provincial thinking like living among others.

Your media must provide broader international coverage so Americans can understand what solutions others have found. Your diplomats and business leaders must be trained in cultural humility, understanding that power without wisdom is merely force. Most importantly, you must create institutions specifically tasked with studying and adapting foreign solutions to American problems.

A Final Warning

When I wrote about America in the 1830s, I said that democracy's greatest danger was its tendency toward tyranny of the majority. Today, I would add another danger: the tyranny of American self-satisfaction.

Remember: The truly great never need to proclaim their greatness. They demonstrate it through wisdom, including the wisdom to learn from others. America's habit of proclaiming its supremacy while ignoring its failures has become its greatest obstacle to actual supremacy.

The choice is yours: Continue to be exceptional in arrogance, or become exceptional in wisdom. You cannot be both.

Chapter 4
The Broken Oath
Hippocrates on the American Healthcare System

I write to you from the shades of Elysium, where we ancient healers gather to observe your modern world. You invoke my name daily in your healing houses, yet I fear you have strayed far from the principles that guided us at the Asclepeion of Kos. What I observe in your healthcare system would have scandalized even the most mercenary of ancient merchants.

The Sacred Art Profaned

In my time, the sick would journey to our healing temples, where they would rest upon clean beds, breathe fresh air, and receive treatment regardless of their status or wealth. The only payment required was what each could afford—sometimes a copper coin, sometimes a chicken, sometimes merely their gratitude. How strange it is to see your temples of healing now transformed into vast mercantile enterprises.

Most peculiar is this entity you call the "insurance company"—a merchant that neither heals nor comforts, yet holds power over both healer and patient. In Athens, such an arrangement would have been seen as hubris of the highest order. Imagine if, in my day, a merchant stood at the temple gates, demanding payment before allowing the sick to enter, or insisted that we use cheaper herbs than those we knew would best cure the ailment. The very notion would have brought shame upon our entire profession.

The Human Cost

Let me share what I recently observed in one of your "emergency rooms." A young mother brought her fevered child for treatment, only to spend precious time arguing with a clerk about whether her particular merchant-guardian would pay for the medicines. In my day, such a delay would have been considered a violation of sacred duty. We understood that Asclepius sent illness without checking one's purse first; why should the cure be different?

This reminds me of an instructive tale from my own practice. Once, a wealthy merchant came to me with a festering wound, offering a bag of gold for treatment. The same day, a slave arrived with an identical ailment but nothing to offer. Both received the same poultice, the same care, the same attention—for disease cares not for social station, nor should its treatment. Yet in your time, I observe with sadness how the quality of care fluctuates precisely with the weight of one's purse.

The Merchants' Triumph

Your "health insurance" system reminds me of the merchants who once tried to sell talismans outside our healing temples, promising protection from disease—charlatans who profited from fear rather than contributing to healing. But while we drove such merchants away with righteous anger, you have invited them into the very heart of your healing practices.

The numbers stagger even my ancient understanding: forty million of your citizens without access to regular care, families bankrupted by medical debt, healers spending precious hours arguing with merchants rather than tending to the sick. Even the wealthy Persians, whom we Greeks often criticized for their excess, ensured their citizens had access to healers!

A Prescription for Reform

Drawing from the wisdom of Asclepius, I see clear remedies for your ailing system. First, healing must be returned to the healers. In our temples, the only voices in treatment decisions were those of the physician, the patient, and the gods. Your healers must be freed from the merchant's yoke to practice their art properly.

Second, the sacred duty of community care must be restored. In Athens, we understood that a city's strength lay in the health of all its citizens, not merely the wealthy. Through public funding of healing temples and the training of physicians, we ensured that none would suffer needlessly.

Third, the healer's true role must be revived. A physician's duty is to ease suffering and promote health, not to serve as a merchant's bookkeeper. Let your healers spend their time with patients rather than with paperwork.

Finally, remember that prevention surpasses cure. We taught the importance of proper diet, exercise, and clean living—what you now call "preventive care." Yet your system seems designed to address illness only once it becomes severe and costly.

A Final Word

Your nation's genius for innovation and progress is unquestionable. You have created healing tools that we in ancient Greece could scarcely have imagined. Yet what good are miraculous treatments if they remain out of reach for so many? A system that denies care to the poor while enriching merchants is not merely inefficient—it is an offense against the healing arts themselves.

Remember: The rod of Asclepius bears no coin purse on its staff. The serpent of healing wisdom winds around a simple walking stick, not a merchant's scales. Let this image guide you as you reform your healing practices. For until healthcare is recognized as a sacred right rather than a mere commodity, you cannot truly claim to honor the oath that bears my name.

Chapter 5
Arms and Anarchy
Alexander Hamilton on Gun Violence in America

I write this with peculiar authority, having both lived by the gun and died by it. That fatal morning on the heights of Weehawken, as I faced Aaron Burr's pistol, I could not have imagined how commonplace such violence would become in our republic. The weapon that ended my life was a gentleman's dueling pistol—deadly, yes, but nothing compared to the instruments of mass slaughter that now plague your streets.

You misunderstand me if you think I oppose firearms entirely. I commanded artillery in our revolution, organized militia units, and helped craft the very amendment you now debate with such fury. But there is a world of difference between the measured approach to arms we envisioned and the bloody chaos I now observe.

The Perversion of Liberty

In The Federalist Papers, I argued extensively for balance between individual rights and the public good. Yet you have somehow twisted this into an absurd absolute—as if any restriction on firearms represents tyranny. I remind you that I also wrote extensively about the necessity of public order and the government's duty to secure domestic tranquility.

Let me be blunt: When I penned our arguments for a "well-regulated militia," I emphasized both "well-regulated" and "militia." We did not envision private arsenals capable of overwhelming law enforcement or turning places of learning into killing fields. The right to bear arms was meant to support ordered liberty, not undermine it.

The Mathematics of Massacre

As a man who loved numbers and logic, what I observe today would have stopped me cold in my days as Treasury Secretary. More Americans now die from firearms in a single month than perished in the entire Whiskey Rebellion. Your children practice hiding from gunmen as routinely as mine practiced their letters. You have created, in essence, a domestic arms race where civilians possess weapons that would have astonished even our military commanders.

The Tyranny of Inaction

You fear government tyranny—a concern I well understand, having fought against British rule. But what of the tyranny of inaction? What of the despotism of special interests that block even the most reasonable regulations? In my time, I faced accusations of monarchical sympathies for suggesting a strong federal government. Yet it was precisely this government that I believed would protect citizens from the chaos of unchecked individual interests.

A Federalist Solution

Drawing from my experience in establishing federal authority over currency and commerce, I see a clear path forward through national standards with local enforcement. Just as we established federal oversight of banking while preserving state-level operations, we must create uniform national firearms standards while allowing local enforcement. No more patchwork of laws that allow weapons to flow from lenient jurisdictions to strict ones.

If you insist on citing the Second Amendment, then honor its full meaning. Require proper training, certification, and ongoing demonstration of competence—just as we required of militia members. The right to bear arms must be earned through proven responsibility.

As I demonstrated with the First Bank of the United States, federal financial power can shape behavior. Impose significant insurance requirements on gun ownership. Create tax structures that discourage excessive arsenals while allowing reasonable ownership. Establish robust systems of background checks, mental health resources, and emergency intervention protocols. I built systems to track and manage federal debt; surely you can build systems to track and manage deadly weapons.

A Personal Reflection

My own death came at the hands of a man who, like so many of your modern shooters, felt aggrieved and sought satisfaction through violence. I chose to waste my shot, firing into the air rather than take Burr's life. This decision, though it cost me my life, reflected my belief that there are principles worth dying for.

But I ask you: What principles are served by allowing the continued slaughter of innocents? What liberty is preserved by permitting troubled individuals to arm themselves for mass murder? What freedom is protected when citizens fear gathering in public spaces?

The constitution we crafted was not meant to be a suicide pact. It was designed to create a functioning society where rights and responsibilities balanced each other. Your failure to regulate firearms rationally is not fidelity to our principles—it is a perversion of them.

I urge you to find the courage that seems to have deserted your legislative bodies. The blood of innocents demands action. And if you continue to resist reasonable reform, then you must accept that you bear responsibility for every preventable death that follows.

Remember: I died in a duel defending my principles. What principles are you willing to die for—or more pertinently, what principles are you willing to let others die for?

Chapter 6
The Rigged Game
Theodore Roosevelt on American Inequality

Bully! The game is rigged, and you know it in your bones. Let me tell you a story. In 1902, I sat across from J.P. Morgan himself in the White House, his famous purple nose and fierce mustache quivering with indignation. *"You can't regulate us,"* he thundered. I leaned forward and replied, *"Oh, but I can, and I will."* By heaven, the look on his face!

Yet today, watching your modern billionaires, I find myself missing old Morgan. At least he built railroads and factories. Your tech titans create apps and algorithms while hoarding wealth that would make even the robber barons blush. Three men—Bezos, Musk, and Zuckerberg—control more wealth than the bottom half of all Americans combined. Even Morgan would have considered that excessive, and he was no friend to the common man!

The New Predators

During my famous hunting expeditions, I learned that the most dangerous beast is one that thinks itself untouchable. Your modern monopolists remind me of the grizzly I once tracked in Colorado—powerful, arrogant, and convinced of their invulnerability. Like that bear, they've grown fat and lazy, certain no one can touch them.

The arrogance is breathtaking. When I was president, the copper kings lived well, but they didn't launch themselves into space while fighting against their workers' bathroom breaks. By thunder, today's CEOs pay themselves 350 times their workers' wages—and then have the audacity to claim they can't afford to raise salaries without raising prices. Nonsense and balderdash!

The Privileged Few

Let me tell you about real privilege. I was born to it, surrounded by it, marinated in it like a well-aged venison steak. But in my time, even the wealthy understood they owed something to society. Today's wealthy have created an entirely new system of extraction and avoidance.

Consider this outrage: Warren Buffett—a man I might have actually liked—admits he pays a lower tax rate than his secretary. In my day, we'd have called that highway robbery. Today, they call it "tax efficiency." When I established the first modern income tax, it was simple: the more you earned, the more you paid. Now they've made it more twisted than a rattlesnake in a roller skate.

They call their income "capital gains" to cut their tax bills in half—it's like calling a wolf a house pet. The teeth are just as sharp, but now it pays half the license fee. They hide their money offshore faster than a spooked deer bounds over fallen logs. The Cayman Islands have more registered corporations than people. Even Morgan wasn't that brazen.

The Corruption of Democracy

During my administration, we hunted monopolies like I hunted big game—with patience, skill, and determination. We broke up 44 of them! Standard Oil? We split it into so many pieces, it looked like a buffalo carcass after the wolves got through with it.

But today's monopolists have learned. They don't just buy politicians—they buy entire political parties. They employ more lobbyists than I had Rough Riders, and believe me, they're rougher on your democracy than any Spanish bullet.

You know what really sets my mustache twitching? These modern robber barons call themselves "self-made." Nonsense! They built their fortunes on public roads, using public education, protected by public laws, and supported by public contracts. Then they hide their profits in offshore accounts to avoid supporting the very system that made them rich!

The Path Forward

Like any good hunter, you need a plan to bag your prey. First, close these tax loopholes tighter than a grizzly's grip. By heaven, when a billionaire pays less tax than a butcher, something's rotten in the meat house!

Second, break up these modern monopolies. These tech giants make Standard Oil look like a corner store. Split them up! No company should be too big to regulate or too powerful to control.

Third, restore workers' power. I faced down mine owners in 1902 to get workers a fair deal. Time to do it again. A company's success should lift all boats, not just the yacht crowd.

Fourth, get money out of politics. When I took on the trusts, at least they couldn't legally buy senators by the dozen. End Citizens United! Let democracy be democracy, not an auction.

A Final Charge

I once led the Rough Riders up San Juan Hill against withering fire. Your challenge today requires similar courage. But remember—I wasn't born a trust-buster. I was born to wealth and privilege. I chose to fight for fairness because I saw how an unfair system corrupts everything it touches.

The monopolists of my era at least had the decency to admit what they were. Your modern robber barons hide behind PR firms and charitable foundations while hoarding more wealth than Midas. They're counting on your frustration turning to despair. Don't give them that satisfaction!

Remember what I learned hunting the biggest game—no beast is too big to bring down if you have the courage to face it and the patience to track it. The trusts seemed invincible in my time too—until we made them vincible!

So get angry, but get smart about it. Get organized. And most importantly, get going! There's a great hunt ahead, and the quarry won't wait forever. Bully to the charge!

Chapter 7

The New Industrial Servitude

Frances Perkins on Worker Rights

On March 25, 1911, I watched helplessly as 146 garment workers, mostly young women, died in the Triangle Shirtwaist Factory fire. That tragedy spurred me to fight for worker protections, culminating in my role as Franklin Roosevelt's Secretary of Labor, where I helped create Social Security, minimum wage, overtime pay, and workplace safety standards. Today, I watch with mounting dismay as many of these hard-won protections are stripped away, creating new forms of worker exploitation.

The Modern Triangle Fire

The tragedy I witnessed in 1911 was stark and visible—women jumping to their deaths because factory owners had locked the fire escapes. Today's exploitation may be less dramatic but it is no less destructive. In Amazon's "fulfillment centers," workers suffer injuries from inhuman quotas that would have shocked even the most callous Victorian factory owner. Throughout the gig economy, workers lack the most basic protections we fought to establish. Across America, minimum wage workers labor full-time yet cannot afford rent anywhere in the nation. The deaths may be slower, but the suffering is just as real.

The Erosion of Protection

When we created the minimum wage in 1938, we designed it to ensure a "minimum standard of living necessary for health, efficiency, and general well-being." Today's federal minimum wage of $7.25 represents a cruel joke—less than half its historic purchasing power. The overtime protections I fought for have been systematically gutted. The right to organize, which we enshrined in law, faces sophisticated suppression through corporate tactics that would make the robber barons blush.

The New Servitude

Your modern corporations have created something I never imagined possible: full-time workers who still live in poverty. When I served as Labor Secretary, we assumed that solving unemployment would solve poverty. Today, I observe millions of employed Americans who cannot afford basic necessities. This isn't economic efficiency; it's institutionalized exploitation.

The corporate power we sought to check has not only returned but grown stronger. Companies now routinely transform employees into "independent contractors" to deny basic benefits that we once considered fundamental rights. They manipulate part-time scheduling to avoid providing healthcare. They deploy sophisticated union-busting tactics while shifting profits offshore and pleading poverty to workers. Corporate executives pay themselves hundreds of times their workers' salaries while using company profits for stock buybacks rather than wage increases.

The Path Forward

Drawing from my experience creating worker protections during the New Deal, I see clear paths to reform. First, the minimum wage must return to its original purpose—ensuring a decent standard of living. It should be indexed to inflation and regional living costs. No one working full-time should live in poverty.

Second, we must modernize worker classifications for the modern economy. Companies cannot be allowed to misclassify employees as contractors simply to deny benefits. Labor laws must be updated to protect gig workers. New economic models must not become vehicles for exploitation.

Third, the right to organize must be strengthened and protected. Union-busting must face real penalties. We must restore the balance of power between workers and management that we originally created through the National Labor Relations Act.

Fourth, large employers must be required to either pay living wages or reimburse the public for supporting their underpaid workers through food stamps and other assistance. The public should not subsidize profitable companies' low wages.

Fifth, corporate governance must be reformed to reflect broader responsibilities. Workers should sit on corporate boards, as they do in many European nations. Executive compensation should be tied to worker well-being. The social contract between business and society must be restored.

A Final Word

When we created modern labor protections, many claimed they would destroy American business. Instead, they helped create the most prosperous economy in history. Today's corporate leaders make the same dire predictions about fair wages and working conditions.

Remember: The Triangle fire happened because profit was placed above human life. Today's exploitation may be less visible, but the underlying choice remains the same—will we prioritize human dignity or corporate profit?

Your current system represents everything we fought to eliminate—workers who cannot live on their wages, corporations that treat employees as disposable, the wealthy few enriching themselves at the expense of the working many.

The choice is yours: Continue allowing the emergence of a new servant class of working poor, or restore the protections and dignity of labor that we fought so hard to establish. As someone who helped create America's middle class, I can tell you—no nation stays strong when its workers grow weak.

Chapter 8
The Great Disruption
Alexander von Humboldt on America's Climate Impact

When I first explored the Americas in 1799, I discovered something revolutionary: nature is a web of life, an interconnected system where every part affects the whole. I saw how deforestation around Lake Valencia in Venezuela changed local rainfall patterns. I understood, for the first time in human history, that mankind could alter climate itself.

Today, I look upon the United States with a scientist's eye and a naturalist's heart, and I am horrified. The local changes I documented have become global, and your nation leads this great disruption. While other developed nations move toward sustainability, America remains stubbornly attached to patterns of consumption that threaten the very systems I discovered.

America's Unique Responsibility

Your nation's impact on global climate staggers even my scientific imagination. Each American produces more than twice the carbon emissions of a European. Your nation, with just 4% of the world's population, generates 15% of global carbon emissions. A single American child has the climate impact of 53 Syrian children. The average American home, twice the size of its European counterpart, demands twice the energy to heat and cool. This is not leadership; it is profligacy on an unprecedented scale.

The Corporate Climate Machine

In my travels, I documented how colonial powers extracted resources with no thought for consequences. Today, I see American corporations doing the same, but with technologies far more destructive than anything in my era. Your fossil fuel companies knew about climate change as early as the 1970s, yet spent millions promoting denial. They continue to expand drilling while Europe transitions to renewable energy.

I observe with particular dismay how oil companies make record profits while blocking climate action, how energy firms spend more on lobbying than on clean energy research, how corporations export polluting industries while importing goods, and how banks fund fossil fuel expansion even while claiming to be "green." The colonial exploitation I witnessed pales beside this systematic assault on Earth's climate systems.

The Culture of Consumption

Your society has engineered what I can only call a machine of perpetual consumption. You build houses so large that one American family occupies space that would house four European families. You discard perfectly good products simply because slightly newer models become available. Your food waste alone could feed millions. Your fashion industry produces more clothes in a day than an 18th-century village needed in a year.

This is not prosperity; it is waste institutionalized as culture. The relationship between consumption and climate change that I first observed in local ecosystems now plays out on a global scale through American excess.

Political Paralysis

What truly astounds me is America's unique political resistance to climate science. In my time, when I explained how forest clearing affected climate, even colonial governors listened. Yet today, you remain the only major nation where climate denial is a mainstream political position. Your energy policy changes radically with each administration. States fight federal environmental protections. Corporate interests block even modest climate legislation.

This political paralysis has global consequences. When America withdrew from climate agreements, it gave cover for other nations to slack in their commitments. The nation that should be leading the world's response to climate change instead leads its denial.

The Path Not Taken

The supreme irony is that America could be profiting from climate leadership. Your technological capabilities could revolutionize clean energy. Your entrepreneurial spirit could drive green innovation. Your universities could lead in climate solutions. Your financial markets could fund global transformation.

Instead, you cling to outdated energy systems while China captures the renewable energy market you should be leading. The nation that put a man on the moon now cannot muster the will to save its own planet.

What Must Be Done

Drawing from my understanding of natural systems, I see clear paths forward. Your aging electrical infrastructure needs rebuilding anyway—make it renewable, resilient, and smart. You have the technology and resources; use them. Reform corporate incentives to reward long-term sustainability over short-term profits. Make corporations accountable for their climate impact.

Your housing stock, among the world's least efficient, needs transformation. Create incentives for renovation and efficiency. What you waste in heating and cooling could power smaller nations. Channel your innovative spirit—the same drive that created the internet—into climate solutions. The nation that leads in clean technology will lead the future.

Rather than exporting polluting industries, export clean technology. Rather than resisting global climate action, lead it. You have the capability; what you lack is will.

A Final Warning

When I discovered the interconnected nature of climate, I warned that humans could devastate these systems. I was right, but too early to be heard. Now the evidence is everywhere, and time grows short.

America, you stand at a crossroads. You can continue to be the world's greatest obstacle to climate action, or you can be its greatest champion. You have the wealth, technology, and creativity to lead the world in climate solutions. What you lack, so far, is the will.

Remember: The natural systems I discovered do not negotiate. They do not respect political parties or profit margins. They respond only to actions, and they are responding now. The question is: Will you finally respond as well?

Chapter 9
The Failed Promise
Horace Mann on American Education

When I championed public education in Massachusetts in the 1830s, I called it *"the great equalizer of the conditions of men."* It was more than a slogan—it was my deepest conviction, born from personal experience. As the first Secretary of the Massachusetts State Board of Education, I created the template for American public education. Today, I observe with profound dismay how that template has been twisted into something that neither equalizes nor truly educates.

The Nature of Educational Inequality

The numbers tell a devastating story. School funding varies by tens of thousands of dollars per student based solely on zip code. The poorest districts, which need the most support, receive the least funding and the most inexperienced teachers. Rich districts spend twice what poor districts can afford. When I fought for public education, I insisted it must be available to all, not just the wealthy. Yet you've created a system where a child's educational opportunities depend almost entirely on their parents' address. This isn't just morally wrong; it's democratically dangerous.

The College Obsession

Perhaps your most peculiar failure is the bizarre fixation with university education as the only path to success. In my time, we understood that different talents required different paths. Your European counterparts still understand this. In Finland, students choose between academic and vocational tracks based on their talents and interests. Both paths receive equal respect and support. Instead, you push college on students who would thrive elsewhere, burden millions with crushing debt, and ignore individual talents and inclinations.

Meanwhile, your economy faces critical shortages of skilled tradespeople, technical workers, and practical professionals—the very careers your educational system stigmatizes. You have created a peculiar system where success is measured only by college admission, while genuine talents and practical skills go unvalued and undeveloped.

The Testing Tyranny

Your standardized testing regime represents another fundamental misunderstanding of education's purpose. When I established public schools, we sought to develop character, build citizenship, and nurture individual talents. Today, your students spend countless hours preparing for standardized tests that measure only a narrow band of skills. Teachers tell me they spend more time teaching test-taking strategies than fostering creativity or critical thinking. This isn't education; it's mechanized instruction designed to produce test scores rather than educated citizens.

The Teacher Crisis

The treatment of your teachers particularly appalls me. When I fought for public education, I insisted on well-trained, well-paid teachers who would be respected professionals. Today, teacher pay is so low that many need second jobs. They face constant testing pressure, limited professional autonomy, and increasing administrative burdens. No society serious about education treats its educators with such disregard. The profession I worked to elevate has been systematically undermined and devalued.

The Path to Reform

Drawing from both my experience creating public education and observation of successful modern systems, I see clear paths forward. First, we must end the practice of funding schools through local property taxes. Create state-level funding mechanisms that ensure every student receives adequate resources, regardless of zip code. The current system perpetuates and amplifies existing inequalities rather than addressing them.

Second, create multiple educational tracks starting in secondary school. Restore and enhance vocational training. Build partnerships with industry for apprenticeships. Stop treating college as the only measure of success. Every student deserves a path to success that matches their talents and interests.

Third, replace the testing regime with meaningful evaluation of student growth and potential. Free teachers to teach rather than prepare for standardized tests. Measure what matters, not just what's easy to measure. Education must nurture the whole person, not just their test-taking abilities.

Fourth, elevate the teaching profession to its rightful status. Increase compensation to professional levels. Restore teacher autonomy in the classroom. Reduce administrative burdens. Rebuild the respect the profession deserves. No education system can rise above the quality of its teachers.

Finally, align education with real opportunity. Create clear pathways between education and employment. Partner with industry to identify needed skills. Prepare students for existing opportunities rather than theoretical futures.

A Final Word

Remember: I called education "the great equalizer" not because it would make everyone the same, but because it would give everyone the opportunity to develop their unique talents and contribute to society. Your system does neither.

The choice before you is clear: Continue pushing everyone toward college while neglecting both excellence and equity, or build a system that values multiple paths, nurtures different talents, and provides real opportunity for all.

As I said in 1848, *"Education is our only political safety."* Today, your educational failures threaten not just individual futures, but democracy itself. The time for fundamental reform is now.

Chapter 10
The Tyranny of Ignorance
John Stuart Mill on American Democracy

Having spent my life examining the delicate machinery of democratic governance, I find myself both fascinated and troubled by the state of your American democracy. In my work "On Liberty," I warned of the dangers of uninformed majority rule. Yet even I could not have envisioned a system where citizens would have unprecedented access to information, yet choose willful ignorance.

The Modern Paradox

Your era presents a peculiar contradiction. Never has knowledge been more accessible, yet never has ignorance been more actively chosen. Your voters carry in their pockets devices that can access the accumulated wisdom of humanity, yet many prefer to consume what I would call the "lower pleasures" of political discourse—inflammatory memes, superficial soundbites, and carefully crafted deceptions.

When I served in Parliament, I observed how even educated voters could be swayed by appeals to passion over reason. But your modern political landscape has industrialized this weakness. Social media algorithms—those mechanical arbiters of information—seem designed to amplify emotion and suppress rational discourse, creating what I feared most: a tyranny of the majority founded on ignorance rather than wisdom.

The Corruption of Discourse

In my writings, I argued that truth emerges from the collision of competing ideas in free and open debate. Yet your "marketplace of ideas" has become a bazaar of deliberate misinformation. Voters are not choosing between competing visions based on facts and reason; they are choosing between competing narratives designed to bypass critical thinking entirely.

I observe your presidential debates with particular dismay. When I debated in the House of Commons, even our fiercest arguments were grounded in policy and principle. Your debates have devolved into spectacles of personality, where substance is sacrificed for soundbites, and complex policies are reduced to slogans that fit on caps. This is not democratic discourse; it is democratic decay.

The Crisis of Competence

Let me be clear: I have always supported universal suffrage. But I also believed it must be paired with universal education—not just in literacy and numeracy, but in the skills of citizenship. Your voters are asked to make decisions about complex issues—monetary policy, international relations, environmental regulations—yet many lack the basic knowledge to evaluate these matters.

This is not, as some suggest, an argument for restricting the franchise. Rather, it is an indictment of a system that has failed to prepare citizens for their democratic responsibilities. A democracy that does not educate its citizens for citizenship inevitably educates them for manipulation.

The Path to Reform

Drawing from my philosophical works and political experience, I see clear paths forward. First, education must be restored to its true purpose—not mere job training, but what I called the cultivation of "higher pleasures"—the ability to think critically, evaluate evidence, and engage with complex ideas. Your schools must teach not just what to think, but how to think.

Second, your information systems require not censorship, but fundamental restructuring to promote thoughtful discourse over emotional manipulation. Perhaps financial incentives could reward depth over clickbait, substance over sensation.

Third, public discourse must be revived in modern form. Not the echo chambers of your current media, but spaces where diverse views must genuinely engage. Disagreement must become respectful and productive again.

Fourth, while the vote must remain universal, create social and economic incentives for civic education. The right to vote must be matched by the responsibility to vote wisely.

Fifth, combat what I termed the "despotism of custom"—the tendency to accept received opinions without examination. Citizens must be encouraged to question their assumptions and seek out opposing views.

A Final Warning

I once wrote that a democracy's quality depends not on its voting mechanisms but on the quality of its voters. Your system has focused obsessively on voting access while neglecting voter competence. Both are essential. A democratic society that neglects either will eventually lose both.

Remember: I championed democracy not because I believed the majority was always right, but because I believed in humanity's capacity for rational self-governance. That capacity must be developed and maintained through education, discourse, and constant vigilance against the forces of ignorance.

Your republic's fate rests not just on protecting the right to vote, but on cultivating the wisdom to vote well. The choice is yours: remain a democracy of impulse and emotion, or become the democracy of reason and enlightenment that your founders - and I - envisioned.

Chapter 11
The Price of the Ticket
James Baldwin on American Racism

Let me speak to you with the same honesty I have always employed. When I left America for Paris in 1948, I was running for my life. When I look at America today, I see that same desperate race continues for too many of your children. The names have changed—from Emmett Till to Trayvon Martin to George Floyd—but the essential American reality has not.

The Persistence of Denial

You tell yourselves a story about progress. Look, you say, we had a Black president. Look at our Black CEOs, our Black celebrities. As though a few successful Black faces in high places somehow negates the reality of your police statistics, your prison populations, your segregated schools and neighborhoods. This is not progress; this is decoration.

Let me be clear: The problem of racism in America has never been simply about hatred. It has always been about power and, more importantly, about identity. White Americans created the "Negro problem" because they needed it—needed it to maintain a particular story about themselves. That has not changed. You have merely learned to speak about it in more sophisticated ways.

The Cost of Self-Deception

When I wrote about the "fire next time," I was speaking of the price America would pay for its continued self-deception. You are paying that price now, though you pretend not to notice. Look at your politics, your social media, your gated communities. You have created a society so fractured by racial anxiety that you can no longer even agree on basic facts about your own history.

Your average white family has accumulated eight times the wealth of your average Black family. Your schools are more segregated now than they were in the 1980s. A Black man is six times more likely to be incarcerated than a white man. Maternal mortality for Black women is three times higher than for white women. These are not accidents. They are not remnants. They are features of a system working exactly as designed.

The Mythology of Innocence

White Americans cling desperately to what I called their "innocence"—their ability to believe that they bear no responsibility for this state of affairs. "I never owned slaves," they say. "I don't see color." This innocence is, in fact, their guilt. It is the mechanism by which injustice perpetuates itself.

You have created new terms—"systemic racism," "white privilege," "implicit bias"—but these are often just sophisticated ways of avoiding personal responsibility. They allow you to acknowledge racism in the abstract while denying it in the particular. The vocabulary has evolved while the reality remains unchanged.

The Path Forward

The way forward begins with abandoning your innocence. It has not served you well. You must face your history not with guilt, which is useless, but with responsibility, which is essential. America's racism is not a Black problem to be solved but a white mythology to be abandoned.

Stop performing anti-racism and start practicing it. Your diversity seminars and corporate statements are not change; they are theater. Real change costs something. Are you willing to pay? Your police, your schools, your banks, your real estate practices - these need more than reform. They need fundamental transformation. This means giving up power, not just sharing it.

White Americans must find a way to be white without requiring Black people to be Black—that is, without needing an "other" to define themselves against. This is the heart of the matter. Your identity cannot continue to depend on our subordination.

I have always insisted that love is the key—not the sentimental love of movies, but the tough, demanding love that seeks truth. Love yourself enough to stop lying about your history. Love your country enough to change it.

A Final Word

I love America, even in my rage at what it does to those it calls its citizens. But love is not passive acceptance. When I critique

America, it is not because I hate it but because I know it can do better. You have everything you need to create real change except the will to do it.

Remember: The "Negro problem" has always been a white problem. Racism is not a stain on American identity; it is American identity. Until you face this, nothing will change.

Your country stands again at a crossroads. You can choose, as you have so often chosen, the comfort of your myths. Or you can choose, at last, to become the nation you claim to be.

The fire this time is already burning. The only question is whether it will destroy or transform. The choice, as it has always been, is yours.

Chapter 12

The Republic in Peril

George Washington on Political Violence

When I led a revolution against British rule, I understood the difference between justified resistance to tyranny and mere violence. When I later put down the Whiskey Rebellion as President, I demonstrated that established democracies must resolve differences through law, not force. Today, I observe with grave concern how political violence threatens the very republic I helped establish.

The Nature of the Threat

The assault on your Capitol building on January 6, 2021, would have confirmed my worst fears about faction and division. But this was merely the most visible manifestation of a deeper crisis. Political violence has become increasingly normalized in your society. Death threats against public officials are now routine occurrences. Armed groups intimidate voters and legislators. Citizens speak openly of civil war. This is how republics die—not necessarily through successful coups, but through the gradual acceptance of violence as a political tool.

The Seeds of Dissolution

In my Farewell Address, I warned against "the spirit of party." Today, I observe how partisan division has evolved into something even more dangerous: a complete breakdown of shared reality and mutual trust. When citizens no longer agree on basic facts, when they view their political opponents as enemies rather than fellow Americans, violence becomes increasingly thinkable. Your social media and partisan news sources inflame these divisions at a scale and speed that would have been unimaginable in my time. Even our most inflammatory partisan newspapers could not match the viral spread of extremism I now witness.

The Corruption of Patriotism

What particularly disturbs me is how extremists wrap themselves in the flag of patriotism. As someone who actually built this nation, let me be clear: Patriotism means defending our constitutional order, not threatening it. Those who claim to love America while plotting violence against its institutions understand neither America nor love of country. When I suppressed the Whiskey Rebellion, I demonstrated that even legitimate grievances must be addressed through constitutional means. Today's extremists skip straight to threats of violence, betraying both democratic principles and patriotic duty.

The Role of Leadership

Political violence flourishes when leaders encourage or excuse it. In my first inaugural address, I emphasized the need for unity and mutual respect. Today, I observe political figures who deliberately inflame division for their own advantage, who hint at violence while maintaining deniability, who place party above country. This is not leadership; it is the abdication of leadership's most sacred duty—preserving the constitutional order.

The Path Forward

Drawing from my experience both making and preserving revolution, I see several essential steps. First, we must restore genuine civic education. Citizens must understand what makes democracy work—not just its forms but its underlying principles. When I established this republic, citizens studied these principles deeply. That fundamental knowledge must be restored.

Second, democratic institutions must be strengthened. Election workers, public officials, and democratic processes must be protected from intimidation. Just as I ensured the peaceful transfer of power, you must maintain these crucial democratic norms.

Third, extremist networks, both domestic and foreign, must be combated effectively. In my time, I warned of foreign influence in domestic politics. Today, both foreign and domestic forces use modern technology to promote violence in ways I could not have imagined.

Fourth, political discourse must be reformed to create spaces for legitimate disagreement that don't devolve into threats and violence. The republic requires vigorous debate, not violent confrontation. We must restore the ability to disagree without becoming enemies.

Fifth, leaders who encourage political violence must face real consequences. When I put down the Whiskey Rebellion, I showed that no one is above the law. This principle must be maintained for democracy to survive.

A Final Warning

Remember: I led an armed revolution, then spent my presidency ensuring that future change would come through peaceful democratic processes. I understood both the necessity of revolution against tyranny and the absolute requirement for law and order in a constitutional republic.

The choice before you is stark: Either reaffirm that political change comes through constitutional means, or watch the republic descend into violence and chaos. As someone who bore arms both for and against this nation, I can tell you: Once political violence becomes acceptable, democracy dies.

What you defend is not just a system of government, but the very possibility of resolving differences without bloodshed. This was my greatest legacy to you. Will you preserve it?

Chapter 13

Democracy for Sale

Louis Brandeis on Money in Politics

When I warned that we could have democracy or concentrated wealth but not both, I was considered an alarmist. Today, as I observe the complete capture of your political system by money, I see that I wasn't alarmist enough. The corruption of democracy by wealth that I fought against in my time has evolved into something far more sophisticated and dangerous than even I imagined possible.

The New Corruption

Let me share what would have shocked even the Gilded Age industrialists I once battled. Your Super PACs spend billions on elections. Corporate lobbying exceeds $3.5 billion annually. Dark money flows through untraceable networks. Single donors contribute hundreds of millions. Politicians spend more time fundraising than governing. The average Senate race costs over $10 million. This isn't just corruption; it's the systematic purchase of democracy itself.

Citizens United: A Constitutional Tragedy

As someone who served on the Supreme Court, I am particularly appalled by the Citizens United decision. The notion that corporations are people and money is speech would have astounded the Constitution's framers. This isn't constitutional interpretation; it's constitutional invention to serve wealth. The results are exactly what one would expect: unlimited corporate spending on elections, untraceable dark money flooding politics, public interest drowned by private wealth, politicians responsive to donors rather than voters, and policy shaped by money rather than merit.

The Machinery of Influence

The system you've created is perversely brilliant in its corruption. Politicians must constantly raise money, making them dependent on wealthy donors. This isn't occasional corruption; it's systematic dependency. Your lobbying industry isn't just influence peddling; it's a shadow government with more staff and resources than Congress itself. Super PACs make a mockery of contribution limits, allowing unlimited spending while maintaining the fiction of independence from campaigns. Dark money flowing through nonprofit organizations makes tracking influence impossible—this isn't transparency; it's legalized secrecy.

The revolving door between government and industry creates a permanent class of influence brokers. Public service has become merely a stepping stone to private gain. The entire system has been designed to institutionalize what we once considered corruption.

The Cost to Democracy

The price of this corruption is paid in policies that serve donors instead of citizens. Healthcare is shaped by insurance companies, environmental policy written by polluters, financial regulations crafted by banks, tax laws designed by the wealthy. The public interest is systematically sacrificed for private gain.

When I fought against monopolies and financial concentration, I was called a radical. Yet the problems I confronted pale beside yours. The trusts I fought sought economic power; today's monied interests seek political dominance itself. Consider the difference: In my time, corrupt politicians took bribes. Today, the entire system is designed to make legal what was once criminal. This isn't occasional corruption; it's institutionalized corruption.

The Path to Reform

Drawing from my experience fighting concentrated power, I see clear paths to reform. First, Citizens United must be overturned through constitutional amendment. Money is not speech, and corporations are not people. This fiction must end.

Second, create a system of public campaign financing that frees politicians from dependency on private wealth. The cost of public financing would be trivial compared to the cost of purchased policy.

Third, reform lobbying by banning the revolving door between government and industry, strengthening disclosure requirements, limiting lobbying by former officials, and enhancing enforcement powers.

Fourth, mandate real transparency. Eliminate dark money. Require real-time disclosure of donations. Create a public database of all political spending. Force disclosure of ultimate donors. Democracy cannot function in darkness.

Fifth, implement structural changes: shorter campaign seasons, stricter conflict of interest rules, enhanced enforcement mechanisms, and genuine transparency requirements.

A Final Warning

In my time, I wrote that sunlight is the best disinfectant. But your system has evolved to avoid sunlight altogether. Dark money flows through shadow organizations, while public policy is shaped in private by unaccountable interests.

Remember: Democracy requires that the people, not money, control government. When wealth captures politics, what remains is merely the facade of democracy. You have created a system where votes matter less than dollars, donors count more than citizens, private interest trumps public good, money drowns out voices, and wealth shapes policy.

The choice is stark but simple: Reform this system, or watch democracy become an empty ritual, with real power residing not in the ballot box but in the checkbook. As I said a century ago, you cannot have both democracy and concentrated wealth. Your system proves my point more thoroughly than I ever wished to be proven right.

Chapter 14
The Warning Unheeded
Eisenhower on the Military-Industrial Complex

As I prepared my farewell address to the nation in 1961, I wrestled with how to express my deepest fear for America's future. As Supreme Allied Commander in World War II, I had seen what massive military mobilization could accomplish. As President, I had watched an entirely new kind of military establishment emerge—one that existed in peacetime, fed by an industry that profited from its perpetual growth. I warned the nation about this "military-industrial complex." Today, I observe with profound sadness how that complex has grown far beyond even my gravest concerns.

The Complex Unleashed

When I commanded the largest military operation in history, our goal was clear: defeat Nazi Germany and restore peace. Industry converted to military production for that specific purpose. Once victory was achieved, they would return to civilian production. But today, I see an industrial machine that requires permanent war—or at least permanent preparation for war—to sustain itself.

Your defense spending now exceeds that of the next ten nations combined. You maintain over 750 bases in 80 countries. A single fighter jet program costs more than the entire Manhattan Project that developed the atomic bomb. The Pentagon cannot even pass a basic financial audit. This is not the military readiness I championed; this is profiteering masquerading as patriotism.

The Corruption of Purpose

What troubles me most deeply is how thoroughly the complex has corrupted legitimate defense needs. During World War II, we built what we needed to achieve victory. Today, you build what generates the most profit, what keeps production lines running in key congressional districts, what serves the interests of defense contractors rather than defense itself.

I watched this begin during my presidency. But the system has now perfected itself. Defense contractors donate generously to congressional campaigns. The recipients ensure continued defense spending in their districts. Pentagon officials retire to lucrative industry positions. Industry lobbyists shape military policy. The machine feeds itself while starving other national needs.

The Price of Perpetual War

Your war in Afghanistan lasted longer than World War I, World War II, and the Korean War combined. Not because victory remained just out of reach, but because ending it would have disrupted the profitable status quo. This is what I feared most—war transformed from a terrible necessity into a business model.

The cost extends far beyond the trillions spent directly on war. Your infrastructure crumbles while defense contractors prosper. You cannot fund healthcare reform, but you can always find money for new weapons systems. Education, scientific research, public health—all must compete for resources against a military-industrial complex that never has to justify its demands.

A Path to Restoration

As someone who commanded armies in war and led the nation in peace, I propose these necessary reforms to restore sanity to our defense:

The political-profit cycle must be broken. No defense contractor should be allowed to donate to political campaigns. The revolving door between the Pentagon and industry must be sealed. The corruption of defense policy by profit motives must end.

The Pentagon must face real accountability. No more missing trillions. No more failed audits. No more cost-plus contracts that reward inefficiency. The Department of Defense must be as accountable as any other government agency.

Most importantly, we must redefine security itself. A nation with failing schools, crumbling bridges, and inadequate healthcare is not a secure nation, no matter how many weapons it possesses.

True national security requires domestic strength as much as military power.

A Final Warning

Let me be clear: I am no pacifist. I commanded the largest military force in history. I served as president during the height of the Cold War. I understand the need for military strength. But what I see today is not strength—it is waste masquerading as strength, profiteering masquerading as patriotism, and perpetual war masquerading as peace.

When I warned about the military-industrial complex, I spoke as someone who understood both the necessity of military power and its dangers to democracy when unbridled. Today, I watch as that complex devours resources that could rebuild America, distorts policy to serve profit, and transforms war itself into a business model.

Remember: No foreign enemy could harm America as much as the unchecked growth of this system. The challenge is not foreign armies—it is the corruption of our own institutions by the monetization of military power.

The choice is yours: Continue feeding a system that enriches the few while weakening the nation, or restore the proper balance between genuine defense and domestic welfare that any great nation requires.

Chapter 15
A System in Chaos
Jane Addams on America's Immigration Failure

When I founded Hull House in Chicago in 1889, I learned quickly that helping immigrants succeed required more than just good intentions. Some thrived despite enormous obstacles. Others, despite our best efforts, could not or would not adapt to American life. Today, as I observe your immigration crisis, I see the same complexities magnified by decades of systematic failure to address fundamental issues.

The Nature of the Crisis

Let me be clear: Your immigration system isn't broken—it's non-existent. What you have instead is a perfect storm of dysfunction. Your borders are neither open nor closed, but chaotic. Your laws are neither enforced nor reformed. Your policies satisfy neither security needs nor humanitarian obligations. Your bureaucracy frustrates both legal and illegal immigrants. Your political rhetoric solves nothing but inflames everything.

The result is a system that paradoxically encourages illegal immigration while making legal immigration unnecessarily difficult. It's as if you designed a system to produce maximum frustration and minimum benefit for everyone involved.

The Myth of Simple Solutions

At Hull House, we learned that neither completely open doors nor firmly closed ones served America's interests. Today's advocates on both sides offer similarly simplistic solutions. "Build a wall" ignores why people cross illegally. "Open borders" ignores legitimate security concerns. "Mass deportation" ignores economic realities. "Amnesty for all" ignores rule of law issues. These are bumper sticker solutions to a problem that requires a policy manual.

The Real Failures

Your system fails at every level. Border control falters not because your agents aren't trying, but because you've given them an impossible task: maintain security while processing humanitarian claims with inadequate resources and contradictory directives.

The process for legal entry has become Byzantine in complexity, glacial in speed, prohibitive in cost, and arbitrary in outcome. No wonder people choose illegal entry when the legal path seems designed to frustrate rather than facilitate.

Your integration systems neither help immigrants succeed nor require them to do so. At Hull House, we learned that both assistance and expectations were necessary. You provide neither consistently. Meanwhile, you maintain the fiction that illegal immigrants don't work while building an economy that depends on their labor. This hypocrisy serves no one well.

The Cost of Chaos

This systematic failure extracts a terrible price. Communities are overwhelmed by unexpected arrivals. Immigrants die in desperate border crossings. Children are separated from parents. Law enforcement becomes demoralized by impossible tasks. Public resources strain under unexpected burdens. Social tensions inflame. Human potential goes to waste.

A Framework for Reform

Drawing from my experience with both successful and failed immigration cases at Hull House, I see clear principles that must guide reform. First, security isn't just walls—it's functional ports of entry, efficient processing, and clear procedures. Make legal entry efficient enough to compete with illegal entry.

Second, establish clear rules and enforce them consistently. End the current system where some laws are enforced severely, others ignored completely. Consistency matters more than severity.

Third, acknowledge your economy's labor needs and create legal paths to meet them. Stop pretending you don't need immigrant workers while employing them anyway. This dishonesty corrupts both law and labor markets.

Fourth, provide opportunities but demand participation. At Hull House, we offered English classes but required attendance. The same principle applies broadly. Integration requires both support and expectation.

Fifth, fund immigration services to match their mission. Currently, you demand first-world results with third-world resources. This mismatch guarantees failure.

A Final Word

At Hull House, we saw both immigration's promise and its problems. We learned that success required both opportunity and obligation, both assistance and accountability. Your current system provides neither.

What you need is not an open door or a closed one, but a functional door—one that opens according to clear rules, closes for clear reasons, and operates with clear purpose.

Remember: The question isn't whether immigration is good or bad. It's whether you can create a system that serves national interests, respects human dignity, maintains security, follows consistent rules, and functions efficiently. Currently, you fail at all of these. Until you address these systematic failures, you will continue to have not an immigration policy, but an immigration crisis.

Chapter 16
Wires and Lights in Darkness
Edward R. Murrow on America's Media Crisis

In 1958, I warned broadcasters that television would become mere "wires and lights in a box" if profit drove out purpose. Today, as I survey your media landscape, I see something far worse: a fragmented, polarized information ecosystem that's destroying the very possibility of democratic discourse. Let me speak with the authority of someone who fought both Nazi propaganda and McCarthyite demagoguery. What you face now is different but equally dangerous: the death of shared truth itself.

The Death of Professional Journalism

The collapse of traditional journalism would shock even my most pessimistic predictions. Over 2,500 newspapers have closed since 2005, leaving 60% of American counties without a daily paper. Half of all journalism jobs have vanished. Where once reporters covered every city council meeting and school board decision, now corruption flourishes in darkness, unobserved and unchecked.

This isn't just the death of newspapers; it's the death of informed citizenship. When I started in radio, local newspapers formed the backbone of American journalism. They monitored local government, investigated corruption, and kept communities informed. Today, these crucial functions have largely disappeared, replaced by information deserts where citizens have no reliable way to know what's happening in their own communities.

The New Information Disorder

Your social media platforms and cable news networks have created something I never imagined possible: parallel information universes where facts don't matter and truth is whatever reinforces existing beliefs. When I fought McCarthy, there were still shared facts to appeal to. Today? Reality itself is contested territory, with citizens choosing comfortable lies over uncomfortable truths.

The economics of this new system are perverse. Algorithms promote outrage because anger drives engagement. Lies travel faster than truth because sensation sells better than substance. Division generates revenue while unity goes unrewarded. The system isn't broken; it's working exactly as designed—maximizing profit by minimizing truth.

The Social Media Catastrophe

Social media represents everything I feared about television's potential for manipulation, multiplied exponentially. Echo chambers reinforce existing beliefs while algorithms systematically eliminate exposure to contrary views. Context vanishes, nuance dies, and attention spans shrink to the point where serious discourse becomes impossible.

The human cost is staggering. Civil discourse has collapsed. Communities fracture along information lines. Problem-solving becomes impossible when citizens can't even agree on basic facts. Democracy itself suffers when its citizens no longer share a common understanding of reality.

The Path Forward

Drawing from my experience fighting both commercial pressure and demagoguery, I see several essential reforms. We must save local journalism through tax incentives, public funding models, and community ownership structures. Social media platforms must be reformed to promote truth over engagement, with transparent algorithms and real consequences for spreading misinformation.

Public broadcasting needs reinvigoration and expansion, particularly at the local level. Professional journalism standards must be restored and enforced. Most importantly, we must educate citizens in media literacy and critical thinking, helping them navigate an information landscape more complex than anything we could have imagined in my era.

A Final Warning

When I fought McCarthy, I said "*We cannot defend freedom abroad by deserting it at home.*" Today, you're deserting something equally fundamental: the shared reality that makes democracy possible. Your modern media system not only fails to create informed citizens—it actively works against this essential democratic function.

Remember: No democracy can function without informed citizens. No citizens can be informed without quality journalism. No quality journalism can exist when truth is trumped by profit and entertainment.

The choice is yours: Continue down the path of profitable polarization and amusing ourselves to death, or rebuild the information infrastructure democracy requires. As I said about television, these media instruments can teach, illuminate, and inspire. But they can do so only to the extent that humans are determined to use them to those ends. Otherwise, they are merely wires and lights in darkness.

Chapter 17
A House Divided
John Marshall on the Supreme Court

When I first took my seat as Chief Justice, the Supreme Court met in a basement room, lacking even its own building. Many questioned whether this fledgling institution could stand equal to Congress and the President. Through careful stewardship, we built its legitimacy brick by brick, earning the public's trust through reasoned judgment and steadfast independence. How it pains me, then, to see what has become of this noble institution.

The Shadow of Partisanship

Your modern Court seems intent on squandering the very legitimacy we worked so hard to establish. In my time, I faced a hostile President Jefferson, who would have happily stripped the Court of its authority. Yet we maintained our independence not through brute force but through careful reasoning and strategic restraint. We built consensus. We persuaded through logic rather than power.

Today, I observe with dismay as your justices split along predictable partisan lines, their votes seemingly determined by which president appointed them. Your confirmation hearings have become political theater, with nominees carefully coached to reveal nothing while senators grandstand for their bases. This is not the thoughtful process of selecting jurists that we envisioned.

The contrast with my era is striking. When I lived in the boarding house with my fellow justices, we debated cases over dinner, challenging each other's views, finding common ground. Now your justices retreat to ideological corners, emerging only to issue rigid pronouncements that read more like political manifestos than judicial opinions.

The Ethics of Power

During my tenure, I faced criticism for ruling on cases where I held financial interests. I responded by being transparent about these conflicts and, in several instances, ruling against my own interests to demonstrate that justice stood above personal gain. Yet today's Court resists even basic ethical constraints that bind every other federal judge in the land.

The revelations of luxury vacations, undisclosed gifts, and hidden financial ties would have scandalized my era. A justice whose integrity was questioned could not function effectively. Yet your modern Court seems to regard ethical concerns as beneath its dignity, refusing to adopt a binding code of conduct.

The Shadow of Night

You have created something called a "shadow docket," allowing momentous decisions to be made without full briefing or argument. In my day, even minor cases received full consideration and public explanation. That you would decide fundamental rights in the dead of night, with minimal reasoning, suggests a Court more interested in power than justice.

Meanwhile, your modern Court seems to regard precedent as an inconvenience to be discarded when it conflicts with preferred outcomes. We built the Court's authority in part through respect for precedent, understanding that stability in law breeds confidence in justice. This casual overturning of settled law undermines the very stability we sought to create.

The Path to Redemption

Drawing from my experience in building the Court's authority, I see clear paths to reform. The Court must immediately adopt a binding code of conduct. No justice should rule on cases involving personal benefactors or financial interests. The Court's authority stems from its integrity; once lost, it cannot easily be regained.

The confirmation process must return to substantive evaluation of judicial philosophy. Create a nonpartisan commission to vet nominees before political consideration. The goal should be to identify jurists of genuine wisdom, not reliable political allies.

The shadow docket must be restricted to true emergencies requiring temporary relief. Fundamental rights deserve full consideration and public explanation. Create structures that encourage real dialogue between justices of different perspectives. Perhaps require that draft opinions be discussed in person before publication.

Most importantly, embrace transparency. The Court's legitimacy rests on public trust. Regular financial disclosures, clear recusal standards, and explained decisions should be mandatory, not optional.

A Final Warning

When we established judicial review, we understood its awesome power required equally awesome restraint. We built the Court's authority not through partisan force but through reasoned judgment that commanded respect across political divides.

I warn you: No institution, however mighty, can long survive the loss of public confidence. The Court's power has always rested more on earned respect than constitutional text. Continue down this path of partisan division, ethical lapses, and midnight justice, and you risk destroying not just the Court's legitimacy but the very foundation of judicial review we labored to establish.

The choice is stark: Return to the principles that built the Court's authority, or watch that authority crumble. Unlike the political branches, the Court has no army to enforce its will, no purse to fund its mandates. It has only its legitimacy. And once lost, such legitimacy may never return.

Remember: We built this institution in a basement, with nothing but principle and persuasion. That same basement awaits if you cannot rebuild the public's trust.

Chapter 18

Living Beyond Our Means

Andrew Jackson on the National Debt

By the eternal! When they told me your national debt had reached $36 trillion, I thought they were speaking in tongues. Then they explained that China —yes, China!—owns over a trillion dollars of it. I nearly drew my pistol on the spot, as I did when that madman tried to assassinate me on the Capitol steps.

Let me tell you something about debt. When I took office, they said our $58 million debt was too big to pay off. "Impossible," the bankers sneered, their fancy coats barely containing their smugness. Well, I paid off every damn cent—the only time in your history it's been done. How? By remembering that every dollar of debt is a dollar of servitude.

The Magic Money Illusion

Your Congress reminds me of a rigged card game I once witnessed in Nashville. They keep dealing out money they don't have, betting that somehow the next hand will pay for the last. They've spent $6 trillion on COVID relief alone, nearly $1 trillion yearly on defense, $400 billion just on interest payments last year, and trillions more on programs they can't afford. Like any good gambling house, they have their fancy explanations. "Modern Monetary Theory," they call it. Sounds as trustworthy as the snake oil salesmen I ran out of Tennessee!

The Real Cost to Real People

You want to know what this debt means to you? Every child born in America today owes $100,000 before taking their first breath. That's right—while you're buying diapers, your newborn already owes more than a house cost in my day. Your government pays more in interest than it spends on veterans' care, education, transportation, and scientific research combined! By heaven, even I didn't hate banks this much until I saw these numbers!

The Foreign Trap

What truly sets my blood boiling is the foreign debt. In my time, we fought for independence from European powers. Now you've willingly enslaved yourselves to China! They own over $1 trillion of your debt. When I forced the Second Bank of the United States to its knees, at least it was an American bank. You've sold your birthright to foreign powers for a mess of pottage!

Every morning, America borrows $2 billion more, much of it from overseas. That's not independence. That's not even smart dependency. That's national suicide on the installment plan!

The Path to Freedom

Here's what must be done, and damn the consequences. First, cut spending NOW. Yes, it will hurt. But I once took a bullet in a duel and left it near my heart for 19 years. Sometimes pain is necessary for survival.

Second, reform your entitlements. Your Social Security and Medicare are going bankrupt. Face it like adults and fix it. In my day, we had the courage to make hard choices. Find yours.

Third, audit everything. I didn't trust the Second Bank of the United States, and you shouldn't trust your government's spending. Audit every department, every program, every dollar. Root out waste like I rooted out corruption.

Fourth, implement tax reform that works—not the wealthy's version or the poor's version, but a fair system where everyone pays their share and no one escapes through loopholes. I fought aristocracy in all its forms—financial aristocracy included.

Fifth, face your creditors. Negotiate better terms, especially with foreign lenders. They need your economy as much as you need their money. Bargain from strength, not weakness.

A Final Warning

I was called "Old Hickory" because I was tough as hickory wood and wouldn't break under pressure. Your debt crisis needs similar backbone. Every day you delay makes it worse. Every dollar you borrow puts chains on your children.

Remember: When I paid off the national debt, they said it couldn't be done. They called me a madman, a populist, a danger to the republic. But I proved them wrong. The question is: do you have the same courage? Or will you leave your children a legacy of debt that would make even those old bankers I fought blush with shame?

The choice is yours. But by heaven, make it soon. Even I never faced an enemy as dangerous as compound interest.

Part Two: Systemic Problems

Chapter 19

An Obsolete Compromise

James Madison on the Electoral College

When we gathered in Philadelphia to create the Constitution, no issue troubled us more than how to select the president. Direct election seemed dangerous—we feared an unqualified populist might sway the masses. Letting Congress choose risked legislative dominance. State selection would fragment national unity. After weeks of debate, we created the Electoral College as a complex compromise. Today, I must tell you: this compromise has outlived its purpose and become a danger to the very democracy we sought to create.

The Original Design

Let me speak frankly about our reasoning. We designed the Electoral College to serve multiple purposes. It would provide a buffer against an unqualified demagogue. It would balance the interests of large and small states. And yes—I must acknowledge this moral failing—it accommodated the Southern states' desire to count enslaved persons for representation through the three-fifths compromise.

We expected electors to be thoughtful citizens exercising independent judgment. We anticipated that elections would often result in no majority, throwing the choice to the House of Representatives where careful deliberation would occur. We thought we had created a system promoting both wisdom and balance.

A System Corrupted

What exists today would be unrecognizable to my fellow Founders. Political parties—which we never anticipated—have captured the mechanism entirely. Electors have become mere rubber stamps, legally bound in many states to vote mechanically. The careful deliberation we envisioned has been replaced by automatic operation.

Even worse, the system now routinely produces results contrary to the popular will. Presidents can take office despite losing the national vote by significant margins. Candidates campaign only in a handful of competitive "swing" states, ignoring most of the nation. Citizens in reliably partisan states might as well not vote for all the influence they have on presidential selection.

The Threat to Democracy

This perversion of our design poses a grave threat to democratic legitimacy. When I helped write the Constitution, we understood that a government's authority flows from the consent of the governed. How can consent be meaningful when the system systematically discounts millions of votes based solely on where they are cast?

The consequences extend far beyond election day. Presidents shape their policies to please swing state voters rather than the national interest. Citizens in uncompetitive states grow cynical about participation. The possibility of a major split between the popular and electoral vote looms over every election, threatening a crisis of legitimacy.

The Path Forward

As one of this system's architects, I must now call for its replacement. We need direct national election of the president. The people have proven themselves capable of directly electing senators; they can handle choosing presidents. Every vote should count equally, regardless of state residence. The artificial distinctions created by state-by-state winner-take-all allocation must end.

This will require constitutional amendment. When we wrote Article V, we specifically intended the Constitution to be updated as experience revealed necessary improvements. Experience has revealed the Electoral College to be not just flawed but dangerous to democratic legitimacy.

A Final Word

Remember: When we designed the Constitution, we created mechanisms for its own improvement. We never intended it to be a sacred text immune to change. We designed it to evolve as the nation grew and circumstances changed.

The Electoral College was created for a young nation with limited democratic experience. It now serves neither its original purpose nor democratic principles. As one of its creators, I tell you: It's time for it to go.

You face a clear choice: Maintain an obsolete system that distorts democracy and risks legitimacy, or move to direct popular election of the president. The question isn't whether to change the system, but how quickly you can do so before it produces another crisis.

In Federalist 68, I wrote about creating the best presidential selection system for our time. Your time requires a different system. The fate of democratic legitimacy itself may depend on your willingness to reform what we created.

Chapter 20
The Dead Hand
Jefferson on America's Constitutional Crisis

I wrote that *"the earth belongs to the living."* Each generation should determine its own governing framework rather than being bound by the dead hand of the past. I even calculated that constitutions should be revised every 19 years—the time it took for a new generation to come of age in my era. Today, I observe with deep concern how America has made its Constitution nearly impossible to amend, forcing each new generation to live under rules they cannot adapt to their times.

The Nature of the Problem

Your amendment process has become functionally impossible. In my time, we understood that the Constitution would need regular updating. Indeed, the first ten amendments—your Bill of Rights—were added almost immediately. Today, you haven't passed a meaningful structural amendment in over 50 years. The last amendment of any significance dealt with presidential succession, and that was in 1967.

This is not the stability we sought; it is paralysis masquerading as reverence.

The Founders' Intent

Let me be clear about our original design. We made constitutional amendment difficult enough to prevent hasty changes but not so difficult as to prevent necessary ones. The high bar for amendments was meant to ensure broad consensus, not to make change impossible.

When I wrote that each generation has a right to choose its own form of government, I wasn't being theoretical. I meant it literally. No generation has the right to bind future generations to its rules without their consent.

The Modern Paralysis

Your political division has made reaching the necessary supermajorities for amendment virtually impossible. Changes that enjoy broad public support—like abolishing the Electoral College or guaranteeing equal rights—cannot achieve the required threshold for ratification.

This paralysis forces problematic workarounds. Courts must stretch constitutional interpretation to address modern needs. Presidents rule increasingly by executive order. Congress delegates vast authority to administrative agencies. None of this is healthy for a democracy.

The Price of Rigidity

The cost of this amendment paralysis extends far beyond specific issues. It undermines the Constitution's legitimacy itself. When a governing document cannot be updated to reflect societal changes and needs, it becomes an obstacle to democracy rather than its foundation.

You face problems we never imagined: artificial intelligence, climate change, global terrorism, corporate power that exceeds many nations. Yet you must address these challenges with a constitutional framework designed for an 18th-century agrarian republic.

A Path to Reform

Drawing from my experience as both a revolutionary and a constitutional thinker, I propose these necessary changes:

First, reform the amendment process itself. Create a mechanism that maintains stability while allowing necessary change. This might require a constitutional convention—something we explicitly provided for.

Second, establish regular constitutional review periods. My suggestion of 19 years might not fit your longer lifespans, but some regular schedule of review and renewal is essential.

Third, develop new ratification methods that maintain broad consensus requirements while preventing a small minority from blocking needed changes.

Fourth, create mechanisms for pilot testing constitutional changes at the state level before national implementation.

Fifth, restore the understanding that the Constitution is a living document meant to serve the living, not a sacred text immune to change.

A Final Warning

Remember: When we wrote the Constitution, we were not establishing an eternal framework. We were creating a system of government that we expected future generations to modify and improve.

The choice before you is clear: Either find ways to update your constitutional framework to address modern challenges, or watch it become increasingly irrelevant and ineffective.

As someone who helped create this system while insisting on its periodic renewal, I tell you: Constitutional reverence must not be allowed to become constitutional paralysis. When I said the earth belongs to the living, I meant that each generation must have the power to shape its governing institutions.

You face a paradox: You must amend the Constitution to make it more amendable. The longer you wait, the harder this task becomes. The question isn't whether to undertake this challenge, but whether you have the wisdom and courage to do so before crisis forces change under less favorable circumstances.

Chapter 21

Houses Without Homes

Jane Jacobs on America's Housing Crisis

In 1961, I wrote "The Death and Life of Great American Cities," a book that revolutionized how we think about cities and communities. When New York's most powerful urban planner, Robert Moses, tried to ram an expressway through lower Manhattan, destroying neighborhoods in its path, I led the successful fight to stop him. My victory showed that citizens could defeat misguided "improvements" pushed by powerful interests. I spent my life studying how cities and neighborhoods actually work, as opposed to how planners and bureaucrats think they should work.

Today, as I observe America's housing crisis, I see the same destructive thinking I fought against, but now it comes not just from planners and developers, but from current residents who pull up the drawbridge once they have their piece of the American Dream.

The Nature of the Crisis

The numbers tell a devastating story about this manufactured crisis. The median home price is now six times the median annual income—double what it was a generation ago. Half of young adults live with their parents because they can't afford housing. In major cities, renters spend over 50% of their income just for shelter. It takes decades to save for a down payment, if it's possible at all.

This isn't a natural market outcome; it's a manufactured crisis. We haven't run out of land or materials or construction workers. We've simply made it nearly impossible to build enough housing where people want to live.

The Protection Racket

You've probably heard the term NIMBY - "Not In My Back Yard." These are residents who fight to prevent any new housing in their neighborhoods, all while claiming to protect "community character." How ironic. In my battles against destructive urban renewal, I fought to protect existing neighborhoods from bulldozers. Today, I watch in dismay as current residents use the same language I once used, but for an opposite purpose: to prevent new housing entirely.

These modern-day protection rackets produce predictable results. Housing shortages drive prices skyward. Young families can't move in. Neighborhoods become frozen in amber, preserved but not truly alive. The very community character these residents claim to protect dies a slow death as neighborhoods become museums of their former selves.

The Rules That Prevent Life

Your zoning laws—the rules governing what can be built where—have become a Byzantine system for preventing housing rather than planning it. When I studied cities, I found that the most vibrant neighborhoods mixed homes, shops, and small businesses, with buildings of various sizes and types. Yet your typical zoning laws now forbid exactly this kind of healthy mixture.

Instead, vast areas are restricted to single-family homes only. Apartment buildings are banned. Small neighborhood shops are prohibited. Absurd requirements for parking spaces make new housing needlessly expensive. You've essentially made it illegal to build the very types of neighborhoods that people most want to live in—neighborhoods like Greenwich Village, which I fought to protect.

The Generational Betrayal

This crisis represents a massive transfer of wealth from young to old. Older homeowners block new construction, which drives up the value of their homes. Meanwhile, young families can't afford to buy homes at these inflated prices. Their rent payments consume so much of their income that they can't save for down payments. The wealth gap between property owners and everyone else grows ever wider.

This isn't just economically unjust; it's socially destructive. When young families can't afford to live in a community, that community loses its future. Schools close for lack of children. Local businesses lose customers. The neighborhood may look the same, but its heart stops beating.

The Path Forward

Drawing from my experience studying successful cities and fighting failed policies, I see several essential reforms. First, we must end the practice of restricting vast areas to single-family homes only. Allow apartments, duplexes, and small condo buildings in all residential areas. Let neighborhoods evolve naturally based on what people need, not what arbitrary rules permit.

Second, enable what we call "missing middle" housing—the duplexes, triplexes, townhouses, and small apartment buildings that historically provided affordable options while maintaining neighborhood scale. Make these housing types legal again.

Third, stop rewarding speculation. Tax vacant land and empty homes at higher rates. Reduce taxes on new housing construction. Make it more profitable to build homes than to hold land empty waiting for prices to rise.

Fourth, strengthen protections for renters. Give them more security in their homes. Create paths from renting to ownership. Stop treating renters as second-class citizens who can be displaced at any landlord's whim.

Fifth, plan for people, not cars. Remove requirements for excessive parking spaces that make housing needlessly expensive. Allow development near public transit. Stop forcing car-dependent design on our communities.

A Final Word

When I fought urban renewal, I said that cities have the capability of providing something for everybody, only because, and only when, they are created by everybody. Today's housing crisis represents the opposite: artificial scarcity created by the few at the expense of the many.

Remember: Cities and neighborhoods are living things that need to grow and change. When we prevent this natural evolution, we don't preserve communities—we kill them. The choice is yours: Continue allowing a privileged minority to block housing for the many, or reform your systems to create genuine housing opportunity for all.

As I observed decades ago, communities decline when they prevent the natural churn of growth and renewal. Your housing crisis isn't just about houses—it's about whether your communities will live or slowly die..

Chapter 22
The Great Stagnation
Baron Haussmann on America's Infrastructure Crisis

When Emperor Napoleon III tasked me with transforming Paris in 1853, I confronted a medieval city choking on its own inadequacies: narrow streets, poor sanitation, nonexistent public transport. Today, I observe American cities facing similar challenges. The difference? Paris allowed me to solve them. America, it seems, prefers to write reports about them.

Let me establish my credentials: I am Baron Georges-Eugène Haussmann, the man who rebuilt Paris into the city you admire today. I created the grand boulevards, modernized the sewers, established public parks, and built an integrated transport system. When Americans visit Paris and sigh with pleasure at its efficiency and beauty, they're admiring my handiwork—while simultaneously accepting infrastructure in their own cities that would embarrass a 19th-century planner.

The American Paradox

Your nation presents a peculiar contradiction. You put men on the moon but can't seem to build a decent train system. You invented the internet but can't maintain your bridges. You lead the world in innovation yet remain stubbornly attached to transportation systems that would have seemed outdated in my time.

Your "high-speed" trains run at speeds my 19th-century locomotives would have mocked. Your urban sprawl makes efficient public transit nearly impossible. Your cities remain enslaved to automobiles while the rest of the developed world embraces alternatives. Your infrastructure receives a grade of C- from your own engineers. This is not progress; this is willing regression.

The Tyranny of the Automobile

When I rebuilt Paris, I designed for the future. You designed for the automobile and now can't imagine anything else. The result? You have created cities where walking is considered exotic, suburbs that require a car just to buy bread, public spaces sacrificed to parking lots, communities divided by highways, and air polluted by millions of individual vehicles. This is not planning; it is surrender to the automobile industry.

The Cost of Inaction

You produce endless studies documenting your infrastructure crisis. Let me save you the trouble with some numbers that would have shocked even my Parisian critics. You have accumulated $2.6 trillion in deferred infrastructure maintenance. You have 45,000 bridges in poor condition. Your citizens waste 6 billion hours annually in traffic congestion. You have zero true high-speed rail lines. Your public transit systems lag decades behind global standards.

The Politics of Paralysis

In my time, I faced fierce opposition to my plans for Paris. But I had two advantages you lack: authority to act and commitment to the future. Your system seems designed to prevent exactly the kind of comprehensive planning and execution that modern infrastructure requires. Projects are split between countless jurisdictions. Funding is held hostage to political whims. Planning is separated from execution. Local interests trump regional needs. Short-term thinking prevents long-term solutions.

The Path Forward

Drawing from my experience transforming Paris, I see clear solutions. First, think systemically. Stop treating infrastructure as isolated projects. Everything connects: transport, housing, commerce, public spaces. Plan accordingly.

Second, embrace public transport. Your addiction to cars is not natural law. Build efficient public transit and people will use it. I know—I proved it in Paris over 150 years ago.

Third, invest in the future. The boulevards I built still serve Paris. Think decades ahead, not election cycles. Infrastructure is for generations, not news cycles.

Fourth, reform planning powers. Create authorities with the power to plan and execute regional solutions. Your fragmented decision-making guarantees fragmented results.

Fifth, change culture. Help your citizens imagine life beyond car dependency. The greatest obstacle to better infrastructure is not cost but conception.

The Price of Leadership

When I transformed Paris, many called me a despot. Perhaps. But I left behind a city that still functions beautifully over 150 years later. What will your current infrastructure leave to future generations?

Consider this: Every other developed nation has high-speed rail networks, modern public transit, well-maintained infrastructure, efficient intercity transport, and walkable cities. Meanwhile, America, the world's richest nation, debates whether such things are even possible.

A Final Word

When I began rebuilding Paris, critics said my plans were too ambitious, too expensive, too disruptive. They were right—and also completely wrong. The cost of doing nothing would have been far greater.

Today, you face a similar choice: Continue to patch your declining infrastructure while falling further behind the developed world, or undertake the kind of comprehensive renewal that the moment demands.

Remember: I transformed Paris from a medieval maze into a modern metropolis in less than two decades. Surely the nation that built the Interstate Highway System in the 1950s can rebuild its infrastructure for the 21st century. The only question is whether you have the vision to see the need and the will to meet it. Currently, I observe plenty of vision studies but precious little will.

Chapter 23

Medicine vs. Handcuffs

William Halsted on America's Drug Policy

Let me speak with the authority of both physician and patient. As one of the founding professors of Johns Hopkins Hospital and a pioneer of modern surgery, I revolutionized medical practice. I also struggled with cocaine and morphine addiction throughout my career—a fact that might shock you, given my professional achievements.

My personal history uniquely qualifies me to address your current crisis. When I became addicted to cocaine while researching its use as an anesthetic, I sought treatment in Europe, later managing my condition while performing thousands of surgeries and training generations of doctors. Today, I would likely be in prison instead of an operating room.

The American Paradox

Your approach to drugs represents a peculiar contradiction that would astonish any medical practitioner. You criminalize addiction while legally prescribing its gateway. You spend billions on enforcement while underfunding treatment. You imprison addicts while failing to address root causes. You treat pharmaceutical companies as legitimate while their practices create addicts. You wage war on drugs while ignoring the war's casualties. The result is a crisis that grows worse despite —or perhaps because of—your attempts to solve it through force.

The Tale of Two Addictions

Consider the opioid epidemic. In my day, morphine addiction was recognized as a medical condition. Today's crisis stems largely from legal prescriptions, yet you respond primarily with criminal enforcement. The numbers are staggering: over 100,000 overdose deaths annually, millions imprisoned for drug offenses, billions spent on enforcement, treatment facilities overwhelmed, communities devastated.

Meanwhile, the pharmaceutical companies that initiated much of this crisis through aggressive opioid marketing face fines they treat as mere business expenses. This would be like allowing a surgeon to continue operating after repeated malpractice, paying only minimal penalties for lives destroyed.

The Failure of Force

Your "war on drugs" has failed by every conceivable measure. Drug availability has increased, potency has strengthened, prices have decreased, usage has expanded, deaths have multiplied, and communities have been militarized. As a surgeon, I learned that treating symptoms while ignoring causes is medical malpractice. Your drug policy represents social malpractice on a massive scale.

The Medical Approach

Drawing from both my professional expertise and personal experience, I see clear paths to reform. First, addiction must be treated as the illness it is. When I struggled with addiction, I continued performing surgery because I received treatment rather than punishment. Your prison-first approach destroys countless potentially productive lives.

Second, the pharmaceutical industry requires stricter regulation than street dealers—their reach is far greater. I developed surgical antisepsis protocols; you need similarly rigorous protocols for prescription opioids. The power to prescribe must come with proportional responsibility.

Third, treatment access must be expanded. In my era, treatment was available to those who could afford it. Today, despite your nation's wealth, treatment remains inaccessible to many. This is both medically unsound and morally indefensible.

Fourth, personal drug use must be decriminalized. Focus law enforcement on large-scale trafficking while treating individual addiction medically. Other nations have proven this approach more effective than mass incarceration.

Fifth, prevention through education must be prioritized. As a medical educator, I emphasized understanding root causes. Drug education should focus on health impacts and risk factors, not just criminal consequences.

Learning from Others

Other nations have shown remarkably more effective approaches. Portugal's decriminalization has reduced addiction rates. Switzerland's heroin-assisted treatment has decreased crime. The Netherlands' harm reduction strategies have lowered death rates. Germany's medical approach has reduced prison populations. Yet America clings to a failed punitive model that even many law enforcement officials acknowledge doesn't work.

A Personal Reflection

Had I been born in your era, my addiction would likely have ended my medical career before it began. Instead, because I was treated as a patient rather than a criminal, I was able to pioneer modern surgical techniques, establish surgical asepsis standards, train generations of surgeons, help found Johns Hopkins Hospital, and advance medical science significantly.

How many potentially productive lives are you losing to prison cells rather than treatment rooms? How many future doctors, scientists, teachers, or artists are we sacrificing to a misguided policy of punishment over treatment?

A Final Word

As both a doctor who treated patients and a patient who required treatment, I understand addiction's complexity. It is a medical condition with social components, not a criminal tendency with medical symptoms.

Remember: When you replace the physician's careful diagnosis with the prosecutor's harsh judgment, you sacrifice both efficiency and humanity. No surgeon would treat a tumor with handcuffs; no nation should treat addiction with prison cells.

The choice is yours: Continue a failed policy of punishment, or embrace a proven approach of treatment. As a surgeon, I learned that the correct treatment, however difficult, is always preferable to the expedient one. It's time America learned the same lesson about addiction.

Chapter 24

The New Asylum

Dorothea Dix on America's Mental Health Crisis

When I began investigating the treatment of the mentally ill in 1841, I found them chained in jails, locked in poorhouse cellars, and forgotten in attics. My exposés led to the creation of the first American mental hospitals, establishing the principle that society has a responsibility to care for its most vulnerable members. Today, I observe with horror how America has recreated the very crisis I fought to solve, just in modern form.

The Return to Darkness

You've closed the hospitals we built and replaced them with nothing. In my time, the mentally ill were imprisoned in jails. Today, your prisons have become your largest mental health facilities. I found people freezing in poorhouse cellars; you have them sleeping on city streets. The faces have changed, but the suffering remains the same. This is not progress; it is the wholesale abandonment of social responsibility disguised as reform.

The Modern Abandonment

What you call "deinstitutionalization"—the closing of mental hospitals—might have been worthy if you had created community alternatives. Instead, you simply abandoned millions to fend for themselves. Those who cannot afford private care end up homeless or imprisoned. Those with insurance face limited coverage and endless barriers to treatment.

When I fought to create mental hospitals, I argued that proper care requires resources and commitment. You've demonstrated neither. Instead, you've created a system where only the wealthy can access adequate mental healthcare, while everyone else suffers.

The Cost of Neglect

The price of this abandonment extends far beyond individual suffering. Your police have become de facto mental health workers, despite lacking proper training. Your emergency rooms overflow with psychiatric patients who have nowhere else to go. Your prisons warehouse the mentally ill at far greater expense than treatment would cost.

I see the same pattern I observed in 1841: Society pays more to neglect the mentally ill than it would cost to treat them humanely. The only difference is the scale of the tragedy. While you've eliminated the physical chains I once fought against, you've created new barriers just as formidable—insurance systems that limit or deny care, shortages of mental health professionals, unaffordable treatment costs, waiting lists that stretch for months, and stigma that prevents people from seeking help. You've replaced iron shackles with financial and bureaucratic ones, while maintaining the same end result: People who need help cannot get it.

The Path Forward

Drawing from my experience creating America's first mental health system, I see clear paths to reform. First, we must restore public mental health infrastructure. Not the warehousing institutions of the past, but modern facilities providing comprehensive care. Every community needs accessible mental health services.

Second, mental health must be integrated into general healthcare. The separation of mental and physical health treatment creates artificial barriers and reinforces stigma. The mind and body cannot be treated separately.

Third, we must train and support more mental health professionals. Your current shortage of providers guarantees that many will go without care. Make it easier to enter mental health professions and provide incentives for serving underserved communities.

Fourth, insurance coverage for mental health must be reformed. Despite laws requiring parity, insurance companies create countless barriers to mental health treatment. This must end.

Fifth, we must address the social conditions that contribute to mental illness. Poverty, isolation, trauma, and stress all impact mental health. Treatment alone cannot solve these broader social issues.

A Final Word

When I began my work, I said that while the public may be indifferent because the mentally ill are concealed from view, "I tell what I have seen." Today, the suffering is visible on your streets, yet indifference remains.

Remember: I proved that reform was possible. Through exposure and advocacy, we built a system of care from nothing. That system had many flaws, but it represented an acceptance of society's responsibility to its most vulnerable members.

The choice before you is clear: Either rebuild a comprehensive mental health system, or continue the cruel abandonment of millions to streets, prisons, and preventable suffering.

As someone who created mental health care in America, I tell you: This crisis is a choice, not an inevitability. You have the resources to provide proper care. What you lack is the moral commitment I once helped inspire.

We built asylums—in the original sense of places of refuge—because society recognized its obligation to care for all its members. You've abandoned that obligation while creating new forms of the very problems I fought to solve. The mentally ill are again imprisoned and abandoned, just in modern ways.

The solution begins with recognizing this fundamental truth: A society that cannot care for its most vulnerable members cannot call itself civilized.

Chapter 25

The New Jungle

Upton Sinclair on America's Food System

When I wrote "The Jungle" in 1906, exposing the horrors of Chicago's meat-packing industry, I said, "*I aimed at the public's heart, and by accident hit its stomach.*" My exposé led to the Pure Food and Drug Act and the Meat Inspection Act. Today, I observe with dismay how America's food system has evolved into something perhaps less obviously grotesque than those early meat-packing plants, but in many ways more insidious and harmful to society.

The Corporate Capture

What I exposed in Chicago was a localized horror. What exists today is a systemic disaster. A handful of massive corporations control most of America's food production. In meat processing alone, four companies control over 80% of beef processing, three dominate chicken production, and four process most of your pork. This concentration exceeds anything the original robber barons imagined possible.

The results are predictable: farmers squeezed to the breaking point, workers exploited, animals mistreated, environment damaged, and consumers harmed—all while corporate profits soar. The greed I exposed in single factories has metastasized throughout the entire food system.

The Subsidy Scandal

Your government subsidizes precisely the wrong things. Billions flow to large industrial farms growing corn and soybeans, much of which becomes either animal feed or processed food ingredients. Meanwhile, fruits and vegetables—what people should eat more of—receive virtually no support. This isn't agriculture; it's corporate welfare that makes healthy food expensive and unhealthy food cheap.

I thought I understood corporate greed in my time. But your system has perfected it: taxpayers subsidize the very foods that make them sick, then pay again through higher healthcare costs. The meatpackers of my era could only dream of such a profitable scheme.

The Nutrition Crisis

Your supermarkets overflow with food, yet millions suffer poor nutrition. Food deserts in poor neighborhoods mean families can't access fresh produce. School lunches prioritize cost over nutrition. Fast food restaurants cluster in low-income areas. The result? A nation simultaneously overfed and undernourished.

When I wrote about hungry workers in "The Jungle," the problem was lack of food. Today, the problem is an abundance of the wrong food, systematically directed toward those with the least resources. The exploitation has become more sophisticated, but no less cruel.

The Environmental Destruction

Industrial agriculture has become a major driver of environmental destruction. Factory farms create massive pollution. Monoculture farming depletes soil. Chemical fertilizers poison waterways. Industrial meat production generates enormous greenhouse gas emissions.

The meat-packing plants I exposed damaged workers and consumers. Today's industrial food system damages the entire planet. The scale of destruction has grown from local to global, but the underlying cause—profit over people—remains the same.

The Path Forward

Drawing from my experience exposing and reforming the food industry, I see clear paths to change. First, use antitrust laws to break up corporate control of food production. Restore competition. Give farmers and consumers real choices. The monopolies I fought were mere babies compared to today's food giants.

Second, redirect agricultural subsidies from industrial commodity crops to fruits, vegetables, and sustainable farming practices. Stop paying farmers to grow crops that harm public health. Make healthy food affordable and accessible to all.

Third, fund local food production and distribution. Eliminate food deserts. Create farmers' markets in every community. Connect local farmers with local consumers. Return food production to human scale.

Fourth, transform school lunch programs into showcases for healthy eating. Use schools to create lifetime good nutrition habits. Support farm-to-school programs. Teach children that food should nourish, not merely fill.

Fifth, regulate industrial agriculture's environmental impact. Support sustainable farming practices. Price food to reflect its true environmental cost. The damage must stop before it becomes irreversible.

A Final Word

When I exposed the meat-packing industry, some defended it as the inevitable price of efficient food production. Today's defenders of industrial agriculture make similar arguments. They were wrong then and are wrong now.

Remember: I said, *"It is difficult to get a man to understand something when his salary depends upon his not understanding it."* Your food system represents this principle perfectly—profits depend on people not understanding how their food is produced or why they're eating what they eat.

The choice is yours: Continue with a system that enriches corporations while damaging health, exploiting workers, and destroying the environment, or build a food system that serves human and environmental needs.

As someone who saw how public exposure could lead to reform, I tell you: The problems are clear, the solutions known. All that's lacking is the will to challenge those who profit from the current system.

Chapter 26
The Illusion of Justice
Cesare Beccaria on America's Death Penalty

When I published "On Crimes and Punishments" in 1764, I demonstrated through reason and evidence that the death penalty serves neither justice nor security. My work helped convince most of Europe to abolish capital punishment. Today, as I observe America's continued embrace of execution, I find myself needing to repeat arguments I made over 250 years ago—arguments that the rest of the developed world has long since accepted.

Let me establish my credentials: I am Cesare Beccaria, the first scholar to systematically analyze criminal justice through the lens of reason rather than revenge. My work influenced your Founding Fathers and helped establish the principle that punishment should deter crime, not merely satisfy vengeance. Yet America, alone among developed nations, clings to a practice that I proved ineffective centuries ago.

The Myth of Deterrence

Let us examine the central claim of death penalty advocates: that it deters crime more effectively than other punishments. I disproved this in 1764 through simple observation: crimes punishable by death continued to occur at similar rates to those punished less severely. Your own FBI data confirms this today. States with capital punishment show no lower murder rates than those without. Some states that abolished the death penalty saw murder rates decline. The highest murder rates often occur in states that execute the most people.

Why does the death penalty fail to deter? I explained this centuries ago: deterrence comes not from severity of punishment but from its certainty and swiftness. A moderate but certain punishment deters more effectively than a severe but uncertain one. Your system of capital punishment, with its decades of appeals and uncertain outcome, could hardly be better designed to minimize deterrent effect.

The Economics of Execution

In my time, I argued that life imprisonment was more efficient than execution. Today, your own data proves this definitively. Capital cases cost states an average of $2.5 million per case, while life imprisonment costs roughly $750,000. The appeals process for death row inmates costs taxpayers millions. States spend hundreds of millions maintaining death row facilities. You are literally spending more to kill people than to keep them imprisoned for life. This is not just morally questionable; it is fiscally irresponsible.

The Problem of Error

I wrote that the death penalty's irreversibility makes it uniquely dangerous in an imperfect justice system. Your experience proves this through stark numbers. Over 185 death row inmates have been exonerated since 1973. For every nine executions, one person on death row has been exonerated. DNA evidence has revealed numerous wrongful convictions. Poor defendants often receive inadequate legal representation. Each exoneration is not just a life saved but proof of the system's fallibility. When the punishment is death, there is no remedy for error.

The Question of Justice

Your Supreme Court has twisted itself in knots trying to make death "humane." They debate execution methods, establish requirements for lethal injection protocols, create rules about mental competency, and set restrictions on executing minors and the mentally disabled. This echoes debates from my era about the "most humane" way to kill. But as I argued then, this misses the point entirely. The issue is not how to kill humanely, but whether the state should kill at all.

The International Isolation

America now stands virtually alone among developed nations in this practice. All European Union nations have abolished it. Canada, Australia, and New Zealand have abandoned it. Japan is the only other developed democracy that still executes. America keeps company with China, Iran, and Saudi Arabia in execution statistics. This isolation should prompt reflection. Why have other nations accepted what I proved centuries ago, while America resists?

The Path Forward

The solution I proposed in 1764 remains valid today. First, replace death with life imprisonment, which provides the same incapacitation effect without the moral and practical problems of execution. Second, invest in crime prevention rather than expensive execution systems. Third, focus on making punishment swift and certain rather than severe. Fourth, target the social conditions that breed violent crime. Fifth, create a system focused on prevention and rehabilitation rather than revenge.

A Final Word

When I wrote in 1764, I faced opposition from those who claimed that ancient practices must be preserved simply because they were ancient. Today, America makes similarly circular arguments for maintaining capital punishment—because it has always done so.

But tradition alone cannot justify a practice that fails to deter crime, costs more than alternatives, risks executing innocents, isolates you from peer nations, and undermines human dignity.

Remember: I demonstrated centuries ago that the death penalty is neither just nor useful. That most of the world has accepted this while America refuses is not a sign of American resolve, but of its resistance to reason and evidence in criminal justice.

The question is not whether America will eventually abolish the death penalty—it will. The question is how many lives and resources will be wasted before it accepts what I proved over 250 years ago.

Chapter 27

In the Dark

Carl Sagan on America's War Against Science

In my 1995 book "The Demon-Haunted World," I warned about a future where America slips into superstition and pseudoscience, where *"clutching our crystals and consulting our horoscopes, we slide, almost without noticing, back into superstition and darkness."* Today, I observe with profound sadness how that warning has become reality in ways even I didn't fully anticipate.

The Scope of Scientific Collapse

The COVID-19 pandemic revealed the depth of this crisis. A significant portion of your population rejected masks despite clear evidence of their effectiveness. Many embraced unproven treatments while refusing tested vaccines. Public health officials faced death threats for presenting scientific data. This wasn't just scientific ignorance; it was active hostility toward scientific thinking itself.

But COVID merely exposed what was already present. Climate change denial persists despite overwhelming evidence. Conspiracy theories flourish. Basic scientific facts about evolution, vaccination, and geology face rejection not based on evidence, but on ideology or political identity.

The Machinery of Anti-Science

What I find particularly disturbing is how modern technology amplifies anti-science thinking. Social media algorithms promote controversy over truth. Cable news networks present scientific issues as political debates. Search engines lead confused people down rabbit holes of misinformation.

When I hosted "Cosmos," I tried to show how science is a way of thinking, not just a body of knowledge. Today, that way of thinking—systematic, evidence-based, open to correction—faces rejection in favor of confirmation bias and emotional reasoning.

The Democratic Cost

In "The Demon-Haunted World," I wrote that science is a vital part of democratic society. Without scientific thinking, citizens cannot evaluate evidence, distinguish fact from fiction, or make informed decisions. Your democracy now suffers exactly these failures.

How can voters assess climate policy without understanding basic science? How can they evaluate public health measures without grasping fundamental biology? How can they judge technical proposals without scientific literacy?

The Path Forward

Drawing from my experience making science accessible while fighting pseudoscience, I propose these essential reforms:

First, transform science education. Stop teaching science as mere facts to memorize. Teach it as a way of thinking, a method for understanding reality. Every student should learn how to evaluate evidence, test claims, and think critically.

Second, reform media coverage of science. Stop presenting scientific issues as two-sided political debates. When 99% of climate scientists agree on human-caused warming, giving equal time to the 1% isn't balance - it's distortion.

Third, create better science communication. Scientists must learn to explain their work clearly to the public. We need more voices making science accessible without dumbing it down.

Fourth, address social media's role in spreading misinformation. Algorithms should not promote conspiracy theories over scientific evidence. Platforms must take responsibility for their role in undermining scientific thinking.

Fifth, restore respect for expertise while maintaining healthy skepticism. As I often said, we need to be skeptical of both authority and skepticism itself. Question everything, but accept evidence when it's strong.

A Final Warning

I once wrote that we live in a society exquisitely dependent on science and technology, where hardly anyone understands science and technology. That dangerous disconnect has grown worse.

Remember: Science isn't perfect. Scientists make mistakes. But science is self-correcting. It's the only system we've found that consistently helps us understand reality and solve problems.

The choice before you is clear: Either restore scientific thinking as a cultural value, or watch your society's ability to address serious challenges continue to erode.

As someone who spent his life making science accessible while fighting superstition, I tell you: This isn't just about science. It's about your society's ability to think clearly, solve problems, and maintain democratic discourse.

We created a civilization based on science and technology. Without scientific thinking, that civilization cannot survive. As I wrote years ago, *"We can judge our progress by the courage of our questions and the depth of our answers."* Right now, too many of you are afraid to ask real questions and unwilling to accept difficult answers.

The consequences extend far beyond science. A society that cannot think scientifically cannot think democratically. The two require the same skills: evaluating evidence, testing claims, changing views based on new information. Lose one, and you'll lose both.

Chapter 28
A Matter of Measure
Condorcet on America's Metric Resistance

Ah, mes amis américains! As a mathematician who helped create the metric system during the French Revolution, I watch with a mixture of amusement and horror as you cling to your imperial measurements like an aristocrat clutching his powdered wig during the Terror.

Let me introduce myself. I am the Marquis de Condorcet, mathematician, philosopher, and revolutionary. When we created the metric system, we sought to overthrow not just political tyranny but also the tyranny of arbitrary measurement. We replaced the chaos of royal measurements—where every French region had its own definition of a foot—with a system based on reason and nature itself.

The American Measurement Regime

And yet here you are, mighty America, still measuring in feet (whose foot?), pounds (which pound?), and gallons (are they

British Imperial or American?). You have sent robots to Mars, split the atom, and mapped the human genome—all using metric measurements, by the way—while your citizens remain trapped in a measurement system as rational as the divine right of kings.

Your contradictions would be comical if they weren't so costly. You buy soda in liters but milk in gallons. Your medicines are measured in milligrams but your food in ounces. Your scientists work in Celsius while your weather reports use Fahrenheit. Your cars show both kilometers and miles, yet you cling to miles. Your Olympic athletes run 100 meters then drink from 12-ounce cans. This is not freedom. This is chaos masquerading as tradition!

The Cost of Chaos

"But Marquis," you protest, "changing would be expensive!" Allow me to introduce you to expensive. Your Mars Climate Orbiter, lost because of confusion between metric and imperial measurements: $327 million. Your industries spend billions annually converting measurements for international trade. Your children waste precious learning time memorizing conversions that shouldn't exist. Your scientists and engineers are forced to work in two systems, risking costly errors.

During our revolution, we calculated that France had over 250,000 different units of measurement. Your system is simpler, but no less arbitrary. Tell me, what is more revolutionary: changing to a rational system once, or permanently forcing every generation to waste time and resources on unnecessary conversions?

The Poetry of Reason

When we designed the metric system, we sought beauty in rationality. Each unit relates to another by simple powers of ten. Water freezes at 0°C and boils at 100°C. One milliliter of water weighs one gram and occupies one cubic centimeter. C'est magnifique!

Compare this to your system: Water freezes at 32°F and boils at 212°F (why these numbers?). A gallon contains 231 cubic inches (naturally!). A mile is 5,280 feet (of course!). Sixteen ounces make a pound, unless they're fluid ounces...This is not a system; it is a collection of historical accidents!

The Path Forward

As someone who believed in both progress and practicality, I see clear steps forward. First, declare your independence from imperial measure. You threw off British political control; why do you maintain their measuring system? Make metric primary and imperial secondary on all labels and signs.

Second, focus on education before implementation. Unlike our revolution, no one needs to lose their head. Teach children metric as primary, imperial as historical. Within a generation, the revolution will be bloodless and complete.

Third, let industry lead the way. Your businesses already use metric for international trade. Make it official. Let commerce lead culture, as it often does.

Fourth, celebrate the rational. Frame metrication as embracing the future, not surrendering the past. You are not losing inches; you are gaining clarity.

Fifth, learn from others' experiences. Every other major nation has made this transition. Learn from their successes and failures.

Even Britain, the source of imperial measures, has largely converted!

A Final Word

During our revolution, I wrote that progress in human rationality was inevitable. Yet here you are, centuries later, still measuring in units that would have seemed arbitrary even to Louis XVI!

America, you champion innovation, yet you measure it with ancient tools. You celebrate freedom, yet you chain yourself to an obsolete system that costs you time, money, and global credibility.

Remember: We created the metric system not just for France, but for humanity. It is not French; it is universal. It is not arbitrary; it is natural. It is not complex; it is elegant in its simplicity.

The choice is yours: Continue to measure the future with tools from the past, or embrace a system designed for precision, clarity, and universal understanding. As we said during our revolution: Progress cannot be measured in half-measures!

Chapter 29
Machines Without Morals
Norbert Wiener on AI Management

When I created the field of cybernetics in the 1940s, studying the relationships between humans and machines, I warned that automated systems would eventually make decisions affecting human lives. I wrote explicitly about the dangers of delegating human judgment to machines without proper safeguards. Today, I observe with mounting alarm how my early warnings have become reality, yet society remains woefully unprepared to manage the technologies it's creating.

The Nature of the Crisis

What I foresaw in theory, you face in practice. Artificial intelligence now makes decisions about who gets loans, jobs, bail, and medical treatment. Automated systems influence what information people see, what they believe, how they vote. Companies deploy AI without understanding its decision-making processes. Society implements these systems without adequate testing or oversight.

When I warned about automation replacing human judgment, some dismissed me as alarmist. Today's reality exceeds even my gravest predictions.

The Abdication of Control

Most disturbing is how you've ceded control of this transformative technology to private corporations driven solely by profit. In my time, I warned specifically about allowing market forces alone to determine the development of powerful automated systems. Yet you've allowed a handful of tech companies to deploy AI technologies that affect billions of lives, with virtually no oversight or accountability.

The race to develop more powerful AI systems proceeds without adequate safety protocols, ethical guidelines, or consideration of societal impact. This isn't innovation; it's reckless endangerment of society's future.

The Human Impact

When I wrote "The Human Use of Human Beings," I emphasized that technology must serve human values and purposes. Today's AI development often does the opposite—humans are forced to adapt to machine requirements. Workers must meet algorithmic quotas. Citizens must navigate automated systems they can't understand or appeal. Democracy itself is threatened by AI-driven manipulation of information and discourse.

This represents exactly what I feared: not machines becoming conscious and taking over, but rather humans surrendering their judgment and autonomy to automated systems through carelessness and greed.

The Path Forward

Drawing from my work in cybernetics and system control, I propose these essential reforms:

First, implement strict oversight of AI development. No automated system should make decisions affecting human lives without rigorous testing, transparent operation, and clear accountability. We require safety testing for new drugs; we should demand no less for AI systems.

Second, establish ethical guidelines for AI development and deployment. These must prioritize human values and rights over technical capability or profit. As I wrote decades ago, the question isn't what machines can do, but what they should do.

Third, create international frameworks for AI governance. No single nation can effectively manage these technologies alone. Just as nuclear technology required international cooperation and control, AI demands global oversight.

Fourth, require transparency in AI systems affecting public life. Any system making decisions about human lives must be explainable and appealable. Black box systems must not be allowed to make black box decisions about human futures.

Fifth, prioritize human agency and dignity. Technology must enhance human capability and freedom, not restrict or replace human judgment. As I argued in my work, machines should serve humans, not the reverse.

A Final Warning

We face a critical moment in human history. AI represents perhaps the most powerful technology humans have ever developed. Yet you're allowing it to evolve without adequate controls, driven by market forces rather than human needs.

Remember: I helped create the mathematical foundations for modern computing and artificial intelligence. I understood these technologies' potential before most. That's precisely why I warned about their dangers.

The choice before you is stark: Either establish meaningful control over AI development now, or face a future where human agency and dignity are increasingly surrendered to automated systems driven by corporate profit rather than human values.

As someone who foresaw these challenges decades ago, I tell you: The window for establishing effective control is closing. Once these technologies are fully embedded in society's critical systems, controlling them becomes exponentially harder. The time for action is now, before market forces and technological momentum make meaningful oversight impossible.

What's at stake isn't just practical control of technology, but the future of human agency and dignity itself. Will you be the masters of your machines, or their servants? The answer will determine not just your future, but the very nature of human society for generations to come.

Chapter 30

The Willing Prisoners

George Orwell on Digital Surveillance

When I wrote "1984", I imagined a world where telescreens watched citizens' every move, thought police monitored their expressions, and Big Brother invaded every aspect of private life. I was wrong about many details, but right about the essence. Your reality proves more insidious than my fiction: you have created a surveillance society more pervasive than anything I could imagine, and most disturbing of all, you did it voluntarily.

The Self-Imposed Telescreen

In my dystopian vision, citizens were forced to have telescreens in their homes. You not only willingly purchase your own surveillance devices, you carry them everywhere. Your smartphones track your location, monitor your activities, and record your conversations. Your smart speakers listen to your home life. Your doorbell cameras watch your neighborhoods. Your social media accounts detail your thoughts, relationships, and daily movements.

The telescreens in "1984" could only watch; yours can predict and manipulate. They analyze your behavior patterns, anticipate your needs, and shape your desires. Most troubling, you've been convinced this invasion of privacy is a feature, not a violation. "Convenience" and "personalization" have become the doublespeak terms for continuous surveillance.

The Corporate Thought Police

I imagined thought police monitoring facial expressions for signs of thoughtcrime. Your reality? Algorithms analyze your every click, purchase, and interaction to predict not just what you think, but what you might think next. Companies track your digital body language with a precision my thought police could only dream of.

The goal isn't merely surveillance but influence. By understanding your behavioral patterns, these corporate watchers can nudge your decisions, shape your opinions, and modify your behavior. The power to predict thought has become the power to direct it.

The New Memory Hole

In my novel, the Party actively rewrote history. Your tech companies accomplish this passively but more effectively. Search algorithms determine what information you easily find and what remains buried. Social media feeds create personalized versions of reality. The past isn't rewritten; it's algorithmically curated, with each person seeing a different version of truth.

Most concerning is how this digital memory hole operates invisibly. You don't see the information you're not shown. You don't know what's been filtered out of your feed. The memory hole has become so sophisticated it disappears itself.

The Surveillance Economy

Perhaps most perverse is how surveillance has been monetized. Your personal information—your interests, fears, relationships, and daily patterns—has become a commodity to be bought and sold. Private companies maintain detailed dossiers that would make my Ministry of Truth envious. Every intimate detail of your lives is collected, analyzed, and sold to the highest bidder.

The economics are elegant in their perversity: the more they watch, the more they learn; the more they learn, the more effectively they can manipulate; the more they manipulate, the more profit they make. Surveillance isn't just profitable—it's becoming the foundation of your economy.

The Path Forward

Unlike in "1984", your surveillance state can still be reformed. But it requires immediate action:

First, recognize surveillance for what it is. Whether done by governments or corporations, monitoring and manipulating human behavior is an exercise of power. "Terms of service" is your newspeak for surrendering fundamental rights.

Second, establish genuine privacy rights. Personal information should be treated as an extension of human dignity, not a commodity to be bought and sold. Digital privacy must become a fundamental right, not a luxury.

Third, break the surveillance economy. Companies must be forbidden from making surveillance their business model. The endless accumulation of personal data must end.

Fourth, restore genuine choice. People need real alternatives to surveillance-based services. Privacy-respecting options must be available and viable.

Finally, rebuild private spaces—both digital and physical. Human development requires room to think, explore, and grow without constant observation. Privacy isn't opposed to security; it's essential to human freedom.

A Final Warning

In "1984", I wrote, "*The choice for mankind lies between freedom and happiness.*" You face a similar choice between convenience and freedom, between personalization and privacy, between the comforts of surveillance and the demands of liberty.

Remember: The telescreens in your pockets are more powerful than any I imagined. They don't just watch—they shape behavior, modify thoughts, and reconstruct reality. Until you reclaim your right to privacy, you remain willing prisoners in a surveillance society of your own making.

The time for action is now, before your voluntary surveillance state becomes as inescapable as the involuntary one I once imagined.

Chapter 31

The Law's Burden

Oliver Wendell Holmes Jr. on America's Litigation Obsession

When I served on the Supreme Court, I wrote that *"the law is not a brooding omnipresence in the sky."* Today, in America, it has become something perhaps worse: a first resort for every grievance, real or imagined. Your society has transformed the courthouse from a last refuge for serious disputes into a universal problem-solving tool, with consequences that would be comic if they weren't so costly.

The Nature of the Problem

The numbers would have astonished even my colleagues on the bench. Your nation has more lawyers per capita than any other, with legal costs consuming 2.2% of GDP. You file 40 million lawsuits annually. Corporate litigation costs average $140 million per billion in revenue. Medical malpractice insurance crushes healthcare providers. Products carry warning labels stating the absurdly obvious, all to prevent lawsuits. This is not a legal system; it is a lottery where every minor mishap is a potential jackpot.

How We Got Here

The path to this predicament was paved with good intentions. You sought to expand access to courts for legitimate grievances, protect consumers from corporate misconduct, ensure compensation for genuine injuries, deter negligent behavior, and promote accountability. But as I once wrote, *"The life of the law has not been logic; it has been experience."* Your experience shows how well-meaning protections can evolve into systemic abuse.

The Costs Beyond Money

The impact of excessive litigation extends far beyond legal fees. Doctors practice defensive medicine, ordering unnecessary tests to protect against lawsuits. Businesses avoid innovation for fear of liability. Public spaces remove amenities to limit exposure. Valuable products are abandoned due to litigation risk. Human interactions are governed by fear of legal consequences. Common sense has been replaced by legal calculation.

When I said that *"the right to swing my fist ends where the other man's nose begins,"* I didn't imagine a society where every accidental contact would trigger a lawsuit. Yet here we are, with personal responsibility replaced by blame-seeking, negotiation abandoned for litigation, and apologies avoided as legal admissions. Risk acceptance has been transformed into risk prosecution, with minor injuries seen as winning lottery tickets and lawyers advertising like personal injury prospectors.

The International Contrast

Other developed nations manage disputes differently. Japan resolves most conflicts through mediation. Germany uses specialized courts and judges, not juries. England follows "loser pays" rules that discourage frivolous suits. Scandinavia employs administrative systems for many claims. Most nations cap damage awards reasonably. Yet America clings to a system that enriches lawyers while often failing both plaintiffs and defendants.

The Path Forward

Drawing from my judicial experience, I see clear paths to reform. First, we must reform damage awards—not to deny compensation, but to ensure it's proportional. As I once wrote, *"Even a dog distinguishes between being stumbled over and being kicked."*

Second, expand alternative dispute resolution. Mandatory mediation for certain cases could resolve disputes more efficiently than trials. The courthouse should be the last resort, not the first stop.

Third, adopt a modified "loser pays" rule—not the full English system, but enough to discourage purely speculative litigation. The prospect of paying the other side's costs would make many think twice before filing frivolous suits.

Fourth, reform class actions to ensure they serve class members, not just attorneys. Current practices often yield minimal benefit to plaintiffs while generating enormous fees for lawyers.

Fifth, create more specialized courts with expert judges for technical matters, reducing reliance on emotional jury appeals. Complex modern disputes require sophisticated understanding.

A Final Word

When I served on the Court, I advocated for viewing law as a practical tool, not a moral absolute. Your experience with unlimited litigation has proven costly, inefficient, and ultimately harmful to the very justice it seeks to serve.

The law should be a shield for the wronged, not a sword for the opportunistic. It should resolve disputes, not create them. It should promote social harmony, not social combat.

Remember: A society where everyone reaches for a lawyer at the slightest provocation is not a society that has achieved justice. It is one that has lost perspective on what justice means.

Chapter 32

Stone Age Banking

J.P. Morgan on America's Financial Infrastructure

"*I want to see the money.*" That's what I told anyone who sought my trust. Today, I look at America's banking system and ask: where IS the money? Lost in a labyrinth of paper checks, antiquated processes, and dollar bills that cost more to print than they're worth. Preposterous!

When I modernized banking, we moved from stagecoaches to telegraphs. Yet here you are, in 2024, still shuffling paper around like medieval merchants. Do you know what I did during the Panic of 1907? I gathered New York's leading bankers in my library and wouldn't let them leave until we solved the crisis. In one night! Meanwhile, your modern banks take longer to clear a check than it once took to ship gold across the Atlantic.

The Absurdity of Your System

In my day, I was called before Congress to defend the efficiency of my banking operations. Today, I would drag your bankers before Congress to defend their inefficiency! The absurdities of your system boggle the mind. While Chinese street vendors accept instant digital payments, you still print paper checks that take days to clear. Your dollar bills last only 18 months before disintegrating, yet you stubbornly refuse to switch to coins. Your banking hours remain stuck in the age of gas lamps, with doors firmly closed on Sundays as if commerce stops for the Sabbath. Most shocking of all, your wire transfers—a technology from MY era—still cost $30 and take days to complete. I built a banking empire on efficiency, and you've built a museum of obsolescence!

A Personal Observation

Let me tell you something about modernization. When I consolidated the steel industry, I eliminated outdated plants and inefficient processes without sentiment or hesitation. Yet your banks cling to paper and antiquated procedures like elderly dowagers clutching their pearls.

I once said, *"A man always has two reasons for doing anything: a good reason and the real reason."* Want to know the real reason your banking system remains in the dark ages? The banks profit from inefficiency! Late fees, overdraft charges, transfer fees—they've built a business model on slowness.

The Cost of Nostalgia

Your attachment to paper currency and checks extracts a staggering toll. Each year, you waste $800 million just printing new dollar bills. Another $2 billion vanishes into the black hole of check processing. Countless hours of productivity evaporate in unnecessary bank visits and payment delays. Billions more disappear to fraud enabled by outdated security measures. When I reorganized railroads, I eliminated every redundant mile of track. Yet your payment systems have more redundant steps than a Virginia reel!

What Must Be Done

Were I to reorganize your banking system, my demands would be clear and non-negotiable. First, eliminate all paper currency under $20, replacing it with coins or digital payments. When I built my empire, we understood that efficiency trumps tradition. Your sentimentality about dollar bills is costly nostalgia.

Second, end this preposterous charade with checks. In my day, checks represented an innovation. Today, they're an artifact. Mandate electronic payments as the default, not the exception. Any banker defending paper checks should be made to personally process them by candlelight.

Third, modernize your transfer systems. Your ACH system is older than television. Build a real-time payment infrastructure like other developed nations. The fact that I can recognize your transfer technology from my era is a damning indictment!

Fourth, create true digital banking. Your "online banking" is just electronic paper pushing. Redesign the entire system for the digital age. When I standardized railroad gauges, I didn't just add new signs to old tracks!

Finally, force innovation through competition. Break up the cozy relationships that let banks profit from inefficiency. I may have created trusts, but at least they were efficient! Your banking oligopoly combines the worst of both worlds—monopoly power with minimal innovation.

A Final Word

In my time, I was criticized for having too much power. But by heaven, I used that power to modernize and streamline American finance. Your modern bankers have similar power but use it to preserve inefficiency for profit.

You know what I told my clients? "*If you have to ask the price, you can't afford it.*" Well, America can no longer afford this antiquated system. The price of your inefficiency is paid in lost time, wasted money, and international competitiveness.

I built a modern banking system for the 20th century. You've let it decay into a steampunk fantasy of paper, delays, and artificial constraints. It's time to demolish this museum of inefficiency and build something worthy of the modern age.

Remember: When Congress asked me if I controlled Wall Street, I replied, "*I don't control it – I just Morgan-ize it.*" Your banking system doesn't need control; it needs Morgan-ization. The question is: who has the courage to do it?

Part Three: Lighter Side

Chapter 33
A Fixed Predicament
Mark Twain on America's Shower Head Folly

I have long believed that civilization is the relentless march toward the improvement of the human condition. We invented fire to keep warm, the wheel to ease our burdens, and indoor plumbing to save us from the horrors of the outhouse. Yet here I stand, dumbfounded, before one of America's most glaring failures of ingenuity: the fixed shower head.

Now, you may think this is a trivial matter, but I assure you it is not. A fixed shower head is the very embodiment of unnecessary hardship. It sprays at a single angle, indifferent to the height or needs of the user. Tall folks crouch; short folks strain; and if you're somewhere in between, you still can't rinse behind your ears without a bit of acrobatics.

Meanwhile, the removable shower head—an invention of grace, flexibility, and pure utility—languishes in the shadow of its inferior cousin. Why? I can only conclude that America, for all its brilliance, has yet to grasp the simple truth that convenience is the cornerstone of comfort.

A National Embarrassment

It is a peculiar thing to excel at sending men to the moon, sequencing genomes, and crafting devices that talk back to you, yet fail to adopt a showering innovation embraced by much of the world. What excuse is there for this oversight? Habit? Stubbornness? A perverse attachment to mediocrity?

Let me paint you a picture: In Europe and much of Asia, the removable shower head is not a luxury but a standard feature. It rinses at any angle, reaches every corner, and offers a level of control that should make any fixed shower head blush with shame. And yet, here in the United States, we cling to the old ways as though a little inconvenience is good for the soul.

The Cost of Inertia

This is not merely a question of comfort; it is a question of progress. The removable shower head offers advantages that are practical, economical, and even ecological. It reduces water waste by directing flow precisely where it is needed. It accommodates the young, the elderly, and everyone in between. It transforms the mundane act of bathing into something resembling an art form. What more could one ask?

And yet, your builders, designers, and homeowners persist with the fixed head, as if to say, "We've suffered this long—why change now?" It is this attitude, this refusal to embrace the better way, that marks a failure of imagination.

A Modest Proposal

It is not too late to redeem yourselves. Indeed, the path to salvation is clear, though it requires the sort of decisive action that Americans typically reserve for matters of far less consequence. First and foremost, we must ban fixed shower heads from new construction entirely. If such mandates are good enough for the metric system, surely they are good enough for this. Set a standard that prioritizes removable heads in every new dwelling, and let no builder dare defy it.

Next, we must incentivize change among the existing homes of our great nation. Offer rebates for retrofits, thinking of it as an investment in national happiness. After all, you subsidize solar panels and electric vehicles—why not the daily comfort of your citizens? A small price to pay for such magnificent returns.

Of course, education must play its part. Many Americans remain tragically unaware of what they are missing, like a person who has never tasted ice cream or heard a symphony. Launch a campaign extolling the virtues of the removable shower head. Let converts share their testimonials. Let the word spread like wildfire until the fixed shower head becomes as obsolete as the horse-drawn carriage.

Finally, and perhaps most importantly, we must make this a matter of national pride. Frame it as a uniquely American opportunity to lead the way in domestic innovation. Declare, boldly, that no nation shall surpass you in the comfort of its citizens. After all, what is American exceptionalism if not the pursuit of a better way of doing things?

Final words

Dear reader, the fixed shower head is a metaphor for all that ails your society: a reluctance to change, a tolerance for mediocrity, and a stubborn resistance to improvement. But take heart—if a nation can rise to abolish slavery, defeat tyranny, and invent the chocolate chip cookie, surely it can conquer the tyranny of the immovable shower head.

So go forth, America, and embrace the removable shower head. Let it be a symbol of your commitment to progress, practicality, and the simple joys of life. And if you still prefer the fixed head, well—perhaps a cold rinse will refresh your perspective.

Chapter 34
Clean Habits and Closed Minds
Benjamin Franklin on America's Bidet Aversion

During my years as America's ambassador to France, I discovered many innovations worthy of adoption by our young nation. The lightning rod, bifocals, and the Franklin stove are among my better-known imports. Yet perhaps the most practical European invention—one that would save resources, improve hygiene, and enhance comfort—remains stubbornly rejected by my fellow Americans: the bidet.

As a man of science and practical improvement, I find this resistance most peculiar. When I proposed daylight savings time, people embraced the idea of adjusting their schedules for efficiency. When I demonstrated electricity's potential, they marveled at the possibilities. Yet suggest a more hygienic and efficient method of personal cleanliness, and Americans react as though you've proposed abolishing apple pie.

A Matter of Practical Philosophy

In my Poor Richard's Almanack, I wrote that *"cleanliness is next to godliness."* Today, I observe with bemusement how Americans champion cleanliness in every aspect of life except this most fundamental one. You insist on daily showers, perpetual hand-washing, and endless loads of laundry, yet cling to a cleaning method that would have seemed primitive even in my day.

Consider the logic: If you got mud on your hands, would you be content merely wiping them with paper? If you stepped in pudding, would you consider your shoes clean after a quick dab with a napkin? Yet when it comes to our most sensitive areas, Americans insist that paper alone suffices. As Poor Richard would say, *"The definition of insanity is using paper to do water's job."*

The Cost of Custom

Your resistance to this practical innovation carries real costs. Americans spend billions annually on toilet paper—a resource-intensive product that clogs pipes, fills landfills, and depletes forests. The environmental impact is staggering: 384 trees must be cut down to supply one person's lifetime toilet paper needs. Meanwhile, you waste countless gallons of water unclogging pipes and washing soiled undergarments.

When I founded America's first fire department, I argued that prevention was better than cure. The same principle applies here. A bidet prevents problems that toilet paper merely pretends to solve. As I wrote about fire prevention, *"An ounce of prevention is worth a pound of cure."* In this case, an ounce of water is worth a pound of paper.

Cultural Mythology

The excuses I hear for avoiding bidets would make Poor Richard blush. Some claim they're "too European"—as though hygiene has a nationality. Others insist they're too expensive—though they cost less than a year's supply of premium toilet paper. Still others claim discomfort with the unfamiliar—the same argument once used against forks and daily bathing.

Having lived extensively in both America and Europe, I can attest that cultural habits, once ingrained, resist change with remarkable stubbornness. Yet as I demonstrated with my Gulf Stream charts, knowledge and enlightenment can overcome even the most entrenched practices.

The Path to Progress

Drawing from my experience in promoting other innovations, I propose a practical path forward:

First, we must normalize the discussion. When I began my scientific investigations into electricity, many considered it too mysterious for public discourse. Through clear writing and practical demonstrations, I made it accessible. The same can be done for bidets. Let us speak plainly about this improvement to daily life.

Second, we should emphasize the practical benefits. Americans are pragmatic people who appreciate efficiency and economy. The bidet saves money, reduces environmental impact, improves hygiene, and increases comfort. These practical advantages should appeal to the American sense of innovation and improvement.

Third, we must make adoption convenient. When I invented the Franklin stove, I ensured it could be easily installed in existing homes. Modern bidets can be added to standard toilets as easily as changing a seat. No renovation required, no plumber needed.

Fourth, we should appeal to American competitiveness. Just as I encouraged Philadelphia to outpace other cities in civic improvements, we should challenge Americans to match global standards of hygiene. Why should any nation surpass us in cleanliness and efficiency?

A Final Reflection

In my autobiography, I wrote of gradually improving myself through practical habits and reasonable innovation. America, too, must continue to improve through practical adoption of superior methods. The bidet represents exactly the kind of practical, efficient, environmentally sound innovation that Americans typically pride themselves on embracing.

Remember: I helped found a nation based on the radical notion that we could improve upon old ways of doing things. Surely, if we could break with monarchy, we can break with outdated hygiene habits. The choice is clear: cling to the wasteful and inefficient past, or embrace a cleaner, more sustainable future.

As Poor Richard would say, "*The definition of folly is rejecting improvement for tradition's sake.*" It's time for Americans to sit down—comfortably—and rethink their resistance to this most practical of innovations.

Chapter 35
The Important Art of Keeping One's Card
Oscar Wilde on American Restaurant Payments

In matters of cuisine, America often attempts to imitate Europe. Usually with the same success as a portrait painter with palsy. Yet nowhere is the charming clumsiness of American dining more evident than in that peculiar ritual that concludes every meal: the ceremonial kidnapping of one's credit card.

A Most Peculiar Custom

In London or Paris, one's credit card, like one's wit, remains present throughout the evening. In America, it is whisked away like a scandalous relative at a society wedding, disappearing into the mysterious depths of the establishment, where one can only hope it isn't being copied by someone with a gambling debt and an entrepreneurial spirit.

The Americans, I've observed, have an extraordinary talent for making simple matters complicated. In Europe, the payment device is brought to you, like the wine list or the day's specials. In America, your financial credentials must apparently undergo a journey of self-discovery, returning eventually with a piece of paper that you're expected to sign while calculating logarithms to determine the appropriate tip.

The Theatre of Trust

"But Mr. Wilde," they tell me, "it's a matter of trust." How fascinating! In a nation that invented the prenuptial agreement and the security camera, trust apparently extends to sending one's credit card on unaccompanied excursions with perfect strangers. This is rather like trusting a fox to guard your chickens while also providing him with cooking instructions.

I recently dined at what claimed to be one of New York's finest establishments. The food was adequate, the wine list pretentious, and naturally, my credit card was invited to tour the premises without me. When I inquired about this practice, the waiter looked at me as if I had suggested we should all dine in the nude—an idea which, I must say, would at least have the virtue of being original.

The Price of Progress

The Americans pride themselves on their technological prowess. They have sent men to the moon, created phones that recognize their faces, and invented social media—that delightful tool that allows one to be simultaneously connected and alone. Yet somehow, the concept of a portable payment device eludes them like good taste eludes a nouveau riche industrialist.

In Europe, even the humblest café possesses these devices. They are not, I assure you, powered by dark magic or requiring advanced degrees to operate. They are simply small machines that prevent your credit card from embarking on adventures without your supervision.

A Modest Suggestion

For those Americans who might wish to join the modern world—and I realize this may be a limited audience—I offer a series of reflections on the art of civilized payment. First and foremost, one must embrace the portable. Your phones may be smart, but your payment systems remain remarkably dim. Portable readers are not merely convenient; they are a sign that one has progressed beyond the financial customs of the Medieval period.

One must also consider the aesthetics of the transaction. There is nothing quite so unattractive as watching one's credit card being carried away like a sacrifice to angry gods. A proper payment should be discrete, elegant, and preferably conducted without requiring one's financial instruments to leave the table—rather like a proper gentleman who knows better than to abandon his companion at dinner.

Moreover, there is the matter of respecting the diner. In matters of dining, as in matters of dress, it is better to be looked over than overlooked. Yet American restaurants overlook the most basic courtesy of allowing their patrons to maintain possession of their own property. It is rather like asking guests to surrender their shoes upon entering the dining room—a practice that, while potentially hygienic, hardly promotes an atmosphere of sophistication.

Finally, if you must imitate European customs, perhaps start with those invented after the printing press. The portable payment device would be an excellent beginning. After all, one should always be thoroughly modern in matters of convenience, even while remaining delightfully antiquated in matters of principle.

A Final Observation

Americans, delightful people though they are, have a peculiar habit of mistaking inconvenience for authenticity. They believe that good service means elaborate ritual, when often it simply means not absconding with your credit card.

Remember: In dining, as in life, it is best to keep your wit sharp, your conversation light, and your credit card where you can see it. Anything else is not sophistication; it is merely habit masquerading as tradition.

As I always say, tradition is merely a successful form of laziness. In the case of American payment customs, it isn't even particularly successful.

Chapter 36
The Patient-Doctor
Molière on America's Pharmaceutical Advertising

In my theatrical career, I thought I had exhausted every possible absurdity of medical practice. My hypochondriacs, quack doctors, and imaginary invalids played out every medical folly known to mankind. Or so I believed, until I witnessed American pharmaceutical advertising—a spectacle so preposterous it would have strained credibility even in my broadest farces.

A Comedy of Modern Errors

Picture, if you will, the scene: A man frolics in a meadow, beaming with unnatural joy while a soothing voice describes his chronic digestive distress. A woman dances through her kitchen, ecstatic about her improved bladder control. These advertisements make my character Argan, who took six enemas a day, seem the very model of medical restraint.

But the true genius lies in the format. The first fifty seconds show these deliriously happy patients, transformed by some miracle drug with an unpronounceable name. Then comes the final ten seconds—a breathless recitation of potential side effects that would make my most murderous stage doctors blush with envy. "May cause sudden death, spontaneous combustion, or an irresistible urge to join the circus. Do not take if you are allergic to things that might kill you."

The Theatre of Medical Absurdity

In my play "The Doctor in Spite of Himself," I created a fake physician who spouted nonsense Latin to impress his patients. How amateurish! Your pharmaceutical companies have perfected this art. They've invented conditions I never knew existed—restless leg syndrome, chronic dry eye, insufficiently glossy hair. Even my hypochondriac Argan never imagined such creative maladies.

The commercials themselves follow a script worthy of classical theatre. Act One: A person suffers from some vague affliction. Act Two: Their doctor, apparently unable to read medical journals, must be told by the patient about a specific brand-name medication. Act Three: Miraculous recovery, accompanied by butterfly migrations and spontaneous family reunions. All this while the side effects—the true Greek chorus of these little dramas—whisper warnings of doom in accelerated speech.

The Economics of Imagination

But perhaps I've been too harsh. These advertisements have accomplished something I never managed in all my plays—they've turned illness into entertainment and medicine into consumer products. Why trust your doctor's education when you can trust a television commercial? Why accept a generic medication when the brand name comes with such lovely background music?

The cost of this entertainment? Merely billions of dollars added to America's healthcare expenses. But what price can you put on the joy of watching middle-aged couples find happiness through proper medication, sitting in separate bathtubs for reasons never quite explained?

The Path to Sanity

The solution is so obvious it could only be American to ignore it. Every other nation on Earth except New Zealand has banned this practice. (And New Zealand, being populated primarily by sheep, may have other reasons for allowing medical advertising.) Stop letting pharmaceutical companies play doctor with the public. Let physicians prescribe based on medical knowledge rather than patient demands inspired by primetime television.

This isn't merely about saving money or medical sense. It's about restoring sanity to the doctor-patient relationship. In my play "The Imaginary Invalid," I mocked those who thought they knew better than their physicians. But even my imaginary invalid never presented his doctor with a list of medications he'd seen advertised between episodes of reality television.

A Final Observation

Remember: When I wrote my medical satires, they were meant to mock the pretensions of 17th-century medicine. Your system has achieved something far more impressive—it has turned my satirical exaggerations into optimistic understatements. You've created a world where patients diagnose themselves based on commercials, then pressure doctors to prescribe accordingly. Even I, who made a career of medical satire, must bow before such magnificent absurdity.

Until this changes, I shall continue to watch your pharmaceutical advertisements with professional admiration. Where I merely wrote comedies about medical folly, you have turned medicine itself into performance art. Bravo, America. Bravo.

Chapter 37

The Path Forward

Finding Hope in Hard Truths

We've heard from some of history's greatest minds about America's problems. Hippocrates diagnosed our healthcare crisis. Hamilton confronted our gun violence. Roosevelt tackled our inequality. Mandela examined our polarization. Each voice brought unique insight to a particular challenge. But stepping back, we can see larger patterns—both troubling and hopeful.

The Heart of the Crisis

Our historical guides, viewing America's problems through different lenses, consistently identified the same core dysfunctions that plague our society. Our institutions have been captured by special interests, their independence compromised, their purposes corrupted. Our decision-making processes have been distorted by money, turning public service into private profit. The very concept of shared reality has eroded, making it impossible to even agree on the nature of our problems, let alone their solutions.

Perhaps most troubling is the loss of our problem-solving capacity. America once tackled huge challenges—electrifying rural areas, building interstate highways, sending humans to the moon. Today, we struggle to maintain existing infrastructure, let alone build for the future. This decline in capability coincides with the triumph of short-term thinking over long-term planning, of immediate profit over sustained progress.

These aren't separate problems but interconnected failures that reinforce each other. This is both bad news and good news. Bad because it means our problems are deeper than they appear. Good because addressing these core issues could help solve multiple problems simultaneously.

The American Paradox

We face a series of stark contradictions that define our current crisis. We possess more wealth than any society in history, yet struggle to fund basic needs. We have access to more information than ever, yet share less common truth. We command more powerful technology than ever imagined, yet watch our infrastructure crumble. We provide more education than previous generations, yet seem to possess less wisdom. We maintain more connections than ever possible before, yet experience less genuine community.

These paradoxes suggest something profound: our problems aren't primarily about resources or capabilities. They're about priorities and processes, about how we make decisions and allocate resources. We have the means to solve our problems but lack the wisdom and will to do so.

Signs of Hope

Despite these challenges, there are reasons for cautious optimism. America has faced and overcome serious challenges before—the Civil War, the Great Depression, the Civil Rights struggle. Each seemed insurmountable at the time, yet each was overcome through determined effort and collective action.

Most of our current problems have known solutions, many proven successful elsewhere. We don't need to invent answers—we need to implement them. More Americans recognize these systemic problems, and younger generations show increasing interest in fundamental reform. We possess unprecedented tools and resources for solving complex problems, if we choose to use them.

The Path to Renewal

Real change requires transformation at multiple levels. Our institutions need fundamental reform—from campaign finance to electoral systems, from regulatory agencies to educational structures. Our processes must be rebuilt to restore long-term planning, public service competence, and fact-based policymaking. Most fundamentally, we need cultural change to rebuild civic engagement, restore faith in collective action, and reestablish a sense of shared purpose.

This transformation begins with citizens demanding better from institutions, supporting necessary reforms, and engaging in civic life. It requires rebuilding community connections and learning to think long-term. Individual actions matter—from getting involved in local government to supporting reform organizations, from demanding better media to engaging in civil dialogue.

The Choice Before Us

America stands at a crossroads. One path leads to continued decay—the slow erosion of our capacity to solve problems and meet challenges. The other path, steeper but ultimately more rewarding, leads to renewal. The choice isn't between left and right, liberal and conservative. It's between dysfunction and functionality, between continued decay and purposeful renewal.

We have the wealth, knowledge, and technology to solve our problems. What we need is the wisdom to use these tools effectively and the will to overcome the interests that resist change.

A Final Word

Hope isn't about believing everything will magically get better. It's about believing that improvement is possible through dedicated effort. The voices in this book didn't just criticize—they acted to solve problems in their own times. Now it's our turn. The challenges are clear. The solutions exist. The tools are available.

Our response will determine not just America's future, but in our interconnected world, humanity's future as well. The stakes couldn't be higher. The time for action couldn't be more urgent. The choice, as always, is ours.

Also by Barry Robbins

Voices of the Civil War
Voices of the American Revolution
Tears of the Titans
Democracy Served Sweet
Three Questions in the Ethereal
The Ethereal Concerto

About the author

Barry hails from Philadelphia and built a career with a prominent international accounting firm, taking him to New York, Washington, D.C., and San Francisco before a new chapter brought him to Finland. He and his Finnish wife adopted two daughters from China, and their family lived in Helsinki for twelve years before he returned to the U.S., now calling Florida home. His years in Finland gave him a new lens through which to view life in America.

Barry's literary work blends satire, history, and whimsy. Known for his Trump satires, including "The Weave", he's earned three gold medals for his sharp wit. His curiosity also led to the Ethereal Bar, a magical place where legends of history stop by for poignant interviews.

Barry's most recent works reveal a thoughtful turn: "Tears of the Titans" examines the regrets of historical icons, while "Voices of the Civil War", "Voices of the American Revolution", and "Voices of Vietnam" bring an immersive, personal lens to these tumultuous periods. With a knack for balancing wit and insight, Barry's writing invites readers to explore history from new, intimate perspectives.

www.ingramcontent.com/pod-product-compliance
Lightning Source LLC
Chambersburg PA
CBHW070626030426
42337CB00020B/3933